THE

TRIUMPH

OF HIS GRACE

*Preparing Ourselves
for the Rapture*

Dedication

This book is dedicated to all those
who love His appearing!

THE TRIUMPH OF HIS GRACE

*Preparing Ourselves
for the Rapture*

by

Paul M. Sadler, Pastor

President, BEREAN BIBLE SOCIETY
Editor, BEREAN SEARCHLIGHT
Radio Teacher, BIBLE TIME
Author, EXPLORING THE UNSEARCHABLE
RICHES OF CHRIST
And other Bible Studies

BEREAN BIBLE SOCIETY
7609 W. Belmont Avenue
Chicago, Illinois 60635

CONTENTS

6

ACKNOWLEDGMENTS

My heartfelt thanks:

To the members and friends of the *Falls Bible Church* who faithfully encouraged me to publish these messages. They will always hold a very special place in this Pastor's heart. May God richly bless these dear saints according to the riches of His grace.

To my family who has patiently endured *another* book. This particular work has given new meaning to the phrase "burning the midnight oil." Once again, as I look up at the clock on the wall it says 12:05 A.M. As a husband, father and a pastor, I am truly grateful for such an understanding family. Surely a great recompense of reward awaits them at the Judgment Seat of Christ.

To my beloved wife, Vicki, who proofread the entire rough draft and meticulously put together the *Scripture Index* that appears at the end of this volume.

To my co-laborer, Richard Hunt, who laid out and typeset the manuscript. Dick is planning to retire soon, so this will be the last book that we will work on together. He began his typesetting career back in the days when they used "hot lead." Imagine his surprise when I walked through the door with a new Macintosh computer equipped with a sophisticated program to do projects such as this. Of course, he nearly had a cardiac arrest! I still recall one of his first comments: "Pastor Sadler, you can't teach an old dog new tricks." "True, I said, but since you're not an old dog I have great confidence that you will master this in two or three weeks!" As you can see, this whole volume was typeset by Dick on that very computer. In fact, he recently purchased one for himself. There is no one more conscientious or capable in the area of typesetting than our Dick Hunt.

To our dear Brother Fred Wisniewski, who between working on the *Berean Searchlight* and a full-time job found time to proofread the entirety of this manuscript. His keen eye and constructive criticism were much appreciated.

—The Author

PREFACE

The doctrine of the *pretribulational Rapture* has long been a bone of contention among those who are serious defenders of the faith. Some dismiss this teaching on the mere grounds that the Rapture of the Church is absent in the pages of Church history; therefore, it is a relatively new doctrine that should be shunned. Then there are those who believe the Rapture is indeed taught in the Scriptures, but fail to see that it is pretribulational. Of course, this has generated a wide array of *unsound theories* namely: *Midtribulationism, Pre-wrath, Posttribulationism, Partial Rapturism,* etc. Moreover, there are those who hold steadfastly that our Lord's coming is pretribulational, but would find it difficult to consistently stand in defense of this precious truth.

We do not deny for a moment that there are many misconceptions in regard to the imminent return of Christ. This does not necessarily mean, however, that it is untrue nor does it negate the fact that the Rapture will be *pretribulational.* Perhaps the thing that has caused the most harm to this Pauline doctrine is the *inconsistent* interpretations by those who deem it to be true. For example, Matthew 24:40,41 is one of the premier passages commonly used by dispensationalists in support of the Rapture. "Then shall two be in the field; the one shall be taken, and the other left. Two women shall be grinding at the mill; the one shall be taken, and the other left." The posttribulationist correctly points out that if these passages teach the Rapture, then it must also be said that it will be posttribulational since they are set in the context of the Second Coming of Christ.

11

By simply rightly dividing the Word of truth, this problem and many others vanish into thin air. This volume addresses the most common criticisms that are raised by those who oppose the pretribulational Rapture. In addition, the author has sought to harmonize the various aspects of this event so those who deem this truth to be self-evident may have a better understanding of our *Blessed Hope*. We trust the reader will be as the Bereans of old, insofar as it was said of them: "These [Bereans] were more noble than those in Thessalonica, in that they received the Word with all readiness of mind, and searched the Scriptures daily, whether those things were so" (Acts 17:11).

INTRODUCTION

The *University of Pittsburgh* is perhaps one of the most highly esteemed schools in Pennsylvania. It has long been known for its academic excellence. When the forty-two story *Cathedral of Learning* was under construction, someone inquired as to why the top of the structure was left unfinished. Not long afterward, this quote appeared in one of the University's publications: "The parallel lines of the truncated Gothic form, never meeting, would imply that learning is unending."

That certainly is a profound statement! But the Scriptures declare that man is *"ever learning, and never able to come to the knowledge of the truth."* In other words, man will *never* come to know God through human wisdom. He must first be *born from above* before he will have the capacity to comprehend the *spiritual* things of God. It therefore behooves us to "be filled with the knowledge of *His will* in all wisdom and spiritual understanding." Of course, this includes "things to come."

If we listen closely, the sound of thunder can be heard in the distance as the coming *day of the Lord* looms on the horizon. As the age of Grace draws to a close, there is an urgent need to tell the unsaved about the Savior so they, too, might flee the wrath to come in the future tribulation. In addition, there is also a sense of urgency to bring those who sincerely desire to know God's Word into a fuller knowledge of the Word, rightly divided. Never before in the recent history of the Church have believers been so confused and unsettled about Christ's coming for His own. Therefore, a great task lies before us to restore the doctrine of the *pretribulational Rapture* to its rightful place of prominence in the canon of Holy Scripture.

The controversy that has raged over this truth of late has a tendency to lessen our joy in this glorious event. Consequently, we pray that God will use this volume to bring much light and blessing to the hearts of the saints in a way that, we trust, will be honoring to Him. The twelve chapters that follow are a comprehensive study on our *Blessed Hope*. With God's help, we shall establish from the Scriptures that those who are the recipients of His grace will be "caught up" *before* the time of Jacob's trouble to forever be with the Lord.

Truly, this shall be the *Triumph of His Grace!* Time may be short! Are you saved? Are you prepared? Are you resting in the promises given to us as members of Christ's Body?

—Pastor Paul M. Sadler

Chicago, Illinois
March 12, 1995

14

1

The Historical Basis for the Pretribulational Rapture

"Now we beseech you, brethren, by the coming of our Lord Jesus Christ, and by our gathering together unto Him."

—*II Thessalonians 2:1*

In 1942, the Japanese devised a plan to launch a surprise attack on Midway Island in the Pacific. This particular battle would prove to be a major turning point of World War II. Of course, Midway was a United States territory. But the Japanese were interested in it primarily because they could use the island as a stepping stone to attack the mainland of America. Admiral Yamamoto of the Japanese fleet knew that he had the upper hand numerically since the Pacific Fleet was nearly decimated at Pearl Harbor. What he did not know, however, was that many of the ships had been repaired and were pressed back into service.

Midway had to be defended no matter what the cost. Thankfully, Admiral Nimitz had a hunch that the Japanese were going to attack somewhere in the Pacific, but he didn't know where or when. About this same time, we had decoded their radio transmissions and it was determined that the attack was on Midway. When the smoke cleared, we had sunk four of their aircraft carriers and severely damaged a number of battleships.

Sometimes we must defend what rightfully belongs to us lest it fall into enemy hands. This is also true in the spiritual realm. A case in point are those who would rob us of the truth of the *pretribulational Rapture.* The past few years have produced a renewed interest in "things to come" that has been unprecedented in recent generations. Many well-meaning teachers of the faith have pointed to the so-called *signs of the times* as evidence that the Lord's return is imminent. We applaud any attempt that encourages the believer to study the Scriptures. However, such an effort can sometimes cause more harm than good if it fails to *rightly divide* the Word of truth.

THE ORIGIN OF THE PRETRIBULATIONAL RAPTURE

"The pretribulational Rapture" is a theological expression that has been adopted over the years to explain two key phrases in Paul's epistles: "delivered us from the wrath to come" and "caught up together" (I Thes. 1:10 cf. I Thes. 4:17). If we dissect the word "pretribulational," the prefix "pre" simply means *before.* The root "tribulation" looks to the future day of the Lord when God will pour out His *wrath* on this Christ-rejecting world (Zeph. 1:14,15). The term "rapture" comes from the Latin word *rapere* of which our English equivalent is "caught up." So then, based on the Scriptures, a good working definition of our phrase would be: Christ will return *preceding* the tribulation period to rapture or *catch away* the Church which is His Body.

16

"And to wait for His Son from heaven, whom He raised from the dead, even Jesus, which delivered us from the wrath to come" (I Thes. 1:10).

Perhaps the most convincing evidence that the Rapture will be pretribulational is the *imminency of Christ's* return. In other words, there are *no* intervening events that must come to pass before the Rapture of the Church —it could take place at "any moment." This cannot be said of the Second Coming of Christ which is closely associated with *signs, times* and *seasons*. Those who will be living at "that day" are instructed to *"Watch* therefore: for ye know not what hour your Lord doth come" (Matt. 24:42). As the sun begins to set over the tribulation, heaven and earth will be arrayed with signs and wonders. Although believing Israel will not know the day or the hour of our Lord's return to earth, they are exhorted to "watch" *after* these signs appear, for their redemption draweth nigh (Matt. 24:29,30; Luke 21:25-28).

In stark contrast to this, the Rapture is a *signless, timeless event* completely unrelated to prophecy. After methodically explaining the many and varied details of our *Blessed Hope* to the saints at Thessalonica, the Scriptures state that Paul exhorted them accordingly: "Wherefore *comfort* one another with these words" (I Thes. 4:18). Surely, the apostle could not have done so had these believers been taught that they were to go through any part of the tribulation. What comfort would there be in that? Paul was able to *console* them on the grounds that their loved ones would rise again and that they would all be gathered together at His *Secret Coming*.

17

Thus, we are exhorted to serve and "wait" until the Lord's return *in the air.* Once again, the apostle instructed his hearers "to wait for His Son from heaven." Please note that the Body of Christ is not to be *waiting* for signs. Rather, we are to *wait* for the Lord. Therefore, those who love His appearing are to be living in *expectancy* of the Savior Himself (Col. 3:4). Why? To be delivered from the *wrath to come!* (I Thes. 1:10; 5:9).

Historically, the recovery of the doctrine of the pretribulational Rapture can, for the most part, be attributed to J. N. Darby at the close of the nineteenth century. We should pause here to add that some have sought to discredit the doctrine of the Rapture on the basis that Mr. Darby had received it from Margaret MacDonald, who was a somewhat questionable source. A product of Pentecostalism, she supposedly received this doctrine through a vision while under the influence of a demon. Margaret MacDonald and Mr. Darby were contemporaries, but there is no credible evidence whatsoever that they ever had contact with one another. Furthermore, no *authentic* documentation or letters have ever been produced to substantiate the above claim. Everything that has ever been written on the matter in support of Margaret MacDonald is mere *speculation.* One need only to study the life and times of J. N. Darby to find that *he* was the student of the Word, not Margaret MacDonald.

Since the rediscovery of this truth has been within the last one hundred and twenty-five years, it has generated a swarm of critics. "Reese, who is usually regarded as the outstanding champion of opponents of pretribulationism, stated categorically that it is 'a series of doctrines that had never been heard of before,' that is, before the nineteenth century. Reese charged that the followers of Darby 'sought to overthrow what, since the Apostolic Age, have been considered by all premillennialists as established results.'"[1]

> "This thou knowest, that all they which are in Asia
> be turned away from me; of whom are Phygellus and
> Hermogenes" (II Tim. 1:15).

While it is true that the doctrine of the Rapture had been a lost gem for many centuries, this teaching has always been an integral part of the Pauline epistles. The reason this wonderful truth was obscure for so many generations was due to the Church's failure to acknowledge the distinctive apostleship and message of Paul. To turn from Paul, as "all Asia" had done, was to reject the apostle's God-given revelation which he had received from the Lord of Glory (I Cor. 14:37; II Tim. 1:15). This, of course, brought the swift judgment of God which plunged Christendom into the Dark Ages. Since then, God has allowed the light of our "Blessed Hope" to shine *again* through the ministry of J. N. Darby and those who have faithfully followed after him. But now, the Church is in danger of falling victim to the same error that caused it to lose this truth in the first place. Sadly, many in our day are following in the footsteps of Phygellus and Hermogenes. As the Scriptures say, "For whatsoever a man soweth, that shall he also reap," and in this case it is *confusion!* With the Church drifting farther and farther away from Paul's message, we have been left with a hodgepodge of views on the

---

1. John Walvoord quoting Alexander Reese in his book entitled, *The Rapture Question,* Chapter 4, Pg. 50.

Lord's return. It is not our purpose to enter into a lengthy deliberation on this matter; however, we do feel that it is important to expose those positions that run contrary to Paul's revelation.

UNSOUND THEORIES

a. Midtribulationism

Advocates of a midtribulational Rapture believe that the Body of Christ will *not* be caught up from the earth until the middle of the future tribulation. This position is based on the premise that none of the events of the first three and one-half years of Jacob's trouble are a consequence of God's *wrath*. Midtribulationists are adamant that the early part of the tribulation is merely the wrath of Satan or man depending on the context. In addition, they believe that certain prophetic events must be fulfilled before the Body of Christ will be removed from the earth. This means that while midtribulationists believe that the *Secret Coming of Christ* and the *Second Advent* are two distinct events, they do not believe that the Rapture is imminent.

Revelation Chapter 11 is usually offered as Scriptural support for this position. In fact, this entire *theory* stands or falls on this passage. The midtribulationist holds that the ascension of the two witnesses in Revelation 11:3-12 is representative of the Rapture. They also insist that the sounding of the seventh trumpet in the Book of Revelation is synonymous with the "last trump" taught in Paul's epistles. In other words, this trumpet marks the "departure" of the Body of Christ and the beginning of the Great Tribulation when God pours out His wrath (Rev. 11:18).

All of these events supposedly transpire in the midpoint of the tribulation, hence the phrase "midtribulational Rapture."

This view is flawed for a number of reasons. First, the two witnesses represent the Law and prophets which ties them directly to the nation Israel (Rev. 11:4-8). Moreover, they pronounce judgment upon their enemies "and if any man will hurt them, he must in this manner be killed" (Rev. 11:5). Both of the above statements are foreign to the Body of Christ. Also, the two witnesses ascend to heaven under the banner of the sixth trumpet; whereas, the midtribulationist claims that the Rapture does not occur until the seventh trumpet is blown. Thus, the Church is removed before the seventh trumpet, which poses a real problem for those who hold this interpretation. Second, dispensationally, the midtribulationist fails to distinguish between Paul's "last trump" (last in a point of time) and the "seventh trumpet" which is the last insofar as *sequence*. We shall go into greater detail on this matter in a later chapter.

b. The Pre-wrath Rapture

Marvin J. Rosenthal has popularized this view in his book entitled *The Pre-wrath Rapture*. Inasmuch as this position is merely a modified form of midtribulationism, we have coined the phrase "the two-thirds" theory. At one time, Mr. Rosenthal was a staunch defender of the pretribulational Rapture. But in more recent days, he has devised an elaborate system of interpretation which places the Rapture at the close of the sixth seal. This is where the plot thickens.

Most dispensationalists believe (ourselves included)

that the *day of Lord* will immediately follow the exodus of the Church. The day of the Lord is an extended period of time that begins with the fulfillment of Daniel's seventieth week. "And he [Antichrist] shall confirm the covenant with many for one week: and in the midst of the week he shall cause the sacrifice and the oblation to cease, and for the overspreading of abominations he shall make it desolate..." (Dan. 9:27). This "week" equals *seven years* and is divided into *two* parts as the passage states. Generally called the *tribulation,* the Scriptures distinguish between the first and second halves accordingly: the beginning of sorrows—*tribulation* and the *Great Tribulation.*

> "All these are the beginning of sorrows. Then shall they deliver you up to be *afflicted,*" [literally, Gr. *thlipsis "to tribulation"*] (Matt. 24:8,9).

> "For then shall be *great tribulation,* such as was not since the beginning of the world to this time, no, nor ever shall be" (Matt. 24:21).

We believe that this *entire period* encompasses the time when God shall pour out His *wrath* upon this Christ-rejecting world (Isa. 13:6-11; Zeph. 1:14-18).

Having said this, Rosenthal departs dramatically from this well-documented and widely accepted conclusion. He states, "It will also be demonstrated that the seventieth week of Daniel has three major, distinct, and identifiable periods of time: the 'beginning of sorrows,' the Great Tribulation, and the day of the Lord—all found in the Olivet Discourse."[2]

The chart that follows illustrates that point.[3]

---

2. *The Pre-wrath Rapture* by Marvin J. Rosenthal, Pg. 61
3. Ibid., Pg. 141

THE DAY OF THE LORD
and the Timing of the Rapture

The Rapture
Cannot Occur
Here . . . .

IF - - - - →

The Day of the Lord
Begins Here.

MIDPOINT

The beginning of Sorrows	The Great Tribulation	**The Day of the Lord**

← 3 1/2 YEARS → | ← 3 1/2 YEARS →

The Rapture Must Immediately Precede The Day of the Lord

—Marvin J. Rosenthal

According to his scheme of thought, Mr. Rosenthal teaches that the *wrath of God* is not manifested until the day of the Lord, which he places approximately "two-thirds" of the way through Daniel's seventieth week. The periods he has adopted preceding this, "the beginning of sorrows" and the "Great Tribulation," are to be associated with *man's* wrath, not God's. He writes, "Prophetically, therefore, the Great Tribulation speaks of man's wrath against man, not God's wrath against man."[4]

While Mr. Rosenthal is a well-respected Bible teacher, we believe that he has missed the mark on a number of fronts.

First, the *day of the Lord* clearly covers the *entirety* of Daniel's seventieth week. When the Apostle John was caught away in the Spirit, he was transported to the future *day of the Lord.* "I was in the Spirit on the *Lord's day,* and heard behind me a great voice, as of a trumpet" (Rev. 1:10). Unlike the Hebrew, in the original Greek language it is possible to translate this phrase in one of two ways, "Lord's day" or "day of the Lord." Tradition says, the "Lord's day" is Sunday, but those who are students of the Word understand that John had the coming *day of the Lord* in mind. Interestingly, he identifies this time as *the tribulation.* "I John, who also am your brother, and companion in [the] tribulation, and in the kingdom. . ." (Rev. 1:9). John then recorded all the events he had *seen* and *heard* in the day of the Lord, beginning with the seven churches in Asia at the commencement of the *tribulation* (Rev. 1:19; 2:1).

Second, the *Great Tribulation* covers the entire second half of Daniel's seventieth week which is a period of three

---

4. Ibid., Pg. 105

and one-half years. This is confirmed by simply comparing the closing words of Daniel's vision with the Olivet Discourse and the Book of Revelation.

As Daniel addresses the latter half of *Jacob's trouble,* he says, "And I heard the man clothed in linen, which was upon the waters of the river, when he held up his right hand and his left hand unto heaven, and swear by Him that liveth forever that it shall be for a *time, times, and an half;* and when he shall have accomplished to scatter the power of the holy people, all these things shall be finished" (Dan. 12:7 cf. 12:1). In prophecy, "time" equals *one,* "times" equals *two,* and "half" is *one-half* of one—hence three and one-half years!

As our Lord delivered the Olivet Discourse, He marked the midpoint of the tribulation with these words: "When ye therefore shall *see* the abomination of desolation, spoken of by Daniel the prophet, stand in the Holy Place. . . . Then let them [Israelites] which be in Judaea flee into the mountains. . . . For then shall be great tribulation. . ." (Matt. 24:15,16,21).

The Apostle John ties all this together for us in Revelation Chapter 12. Inasmuch as there will be so many events occurring in the middle of the tribulation, John spends the better part of four chapters describing them. He, too, confirms that the latter part of the tribulation *(Great Tribulation)* will span 3 1/2 years. "And to the woman [Israel] were given two wings of a great eagle, that she might fly into the wilderness, into her place, where she is nourished for a *time, and times, and half a time,* from the face of the serpent" (Rev. 12:14).

Third, there are three sets of judgments that cover the future tribulation: *seals, trumpets and bowls* (See chart on page 58). As the Lamb opens each of the seven seals, a major catastrophic *event* takes place on the earth. This is the first wave of the *wrath of God,* even if it is only to be understood as God removing His providential care from the earth. May we underscore, however, that God's wrath greatly intensifies as we move through the dreaded time of Jacob's trouble. If the reader places the "beginning of sorrows" revealed in the Olivet Discourse alongside the "seal judgments," you will find that they are identical. In fact, they follow the same order.

The opening of the sixth seal causes the heavens and earth to shake so violently that heaven temporarily rolls up like a scroll and the mountains and islands are *moved* out of their places (Rev. 6:12-14). This disturbance should not be confused with the judgment under the seventh bowl when "every island *fled away,* and the mountains were *not found*" (Rev. 16:18-20). The events of the sixth seal will be so horrific that men will cry out for the rocks to fall upon them to hide them from the wrath of the Lamb.

"For the great day of His wrath is come; and who shall be able to stand?" (Rev. 6:17). The phrase "His wrath is come" is in the aorist tense in the original which normally indicates a *past* action. Thus, those who experience the horrors of these *first* six seals will fully understand that they are a direct result of the *wrath of God.* Remember, these seals transpire in the *first part* of the tribulation and are only the beginning of sorrows. The worst is yet to come!

26

c. **Posttribulationism**

Insofar as there are so many variations to posttribulationism, we shall only state the basic premise of this position fearing we may misrepresent one of its exponents. Those who defend this theory teach that the Church will remain on the earth through the *entirety* of the future tribulation. At the close of Jacob's trouble, the elect will be *caught up* to meet the Lord who has descended into the upper atmosphere on His way to the earth. Consequently, the Church will accompany Him to the earth in His Second Coming. Alexander Reese, an ardent defender of this viewpoint writes:

"The Church of Christ will not be removed from the earth until the Advent of Christ [Second Coming] at the very end of the present Age [Great Tribulation]: the Rapture and the Appearing [Second Coming] take place at the same crisis; hence Christians at that generation will be exposed to the final affliction under the Antichrist."[5]

If the above statement is analyzed carefully, it is clear that posttribulationists deny all dispensational distinctions, even though some in their camp claim to be dispensationalists. In this respect, they do not distinguish between Israel and the Body of Christ; therefore, the posttibulationist believes that the Rapture and the Second Coming are the *same* event. In order to remain consistent with their system of interpretation proponents of this view, also reject the imminent return of Christ, claiming that various signs and wonders must precede the Lord's return.

In addition, posttribulationists attempt to dismiss any

---

5. Alexander Reese, *The Approaching Advent of Christ,* Pg. 18.

thought of a pretribulational Rapture on the grounds that the *first resurrection* is inseparably bound to the Second Coming of Christ in Scripture. Thus they argue, out of necessity, that if the Old Testament saints are raised at the Rapture, then it must be posttribulational in accordance with Revelation 20:6. In his summation on the resurrection, McPherson states:

"Clearly the resurrection of the holy dead takes place at the Rapture of the Church (I Thes. 4:16). Therefore, 'wheresoever the resurrection is, there will the Rapture be also.' Upon examining passages that speak of the resurrection of the holy dead, which is the first resurrection (Rev. 20:5,6), we find that this first resurrection is associated with the [Second] Coming of the Lord (Isa. 26:19), the conversion of Israel (Rom. 11:15), the inauguration of the kingdom (Luke 14:14,15; Rev. 20:4-6), the giving of rewards (Rev. 11:15-18), the Great Tribulation coming before it (Dan. 12:1-3)."[6]

As far as we know, J. N. Darby was the first to place the resurrection of the Old Testament saints at the Rapture. Dr. C. I. Scofield followed suit, which essentially embedded this teaching into the present day Acts 2 position. But not all dispensationalists (including ourselves) adhere to this system of thought. Those who rightly divide the Word of truth hold the position that only the members of the Body of Christ will be resurrected at the Rapture (I Cor. 15:51,52 cf. I Thes. 4:16). On the other hand, the resurrection of the Old Testament saints will occur when Christ returns in His glory to establish the millennial kingdom (Rev. 19:11-16 cf. 20:6). The order of the resurrections will be examined more comprehensively in Chapter 10.

6. Norman S. McPherson, *Triumph Through Tribulation,* Pg. 41

In regard to posttribulationism, Professor Dwight Pentecost makes this interesting observation: "It will thus be observed that the position rests essentially on a system of denials of the interpretations held by the pretribulation rapturists rather than on a positive exposition of Scripture."[7]

d. The Partial Rapture Theory

Little is known about the origin of this particular theory other than it is usually credited to a man by the name of Robert Govett. This view concerns itself more with the *subjects* of the Rapture than it does the relationship of the event to the tribulation. Adherents to this presupposition believe that only those who are *faithful* and *waiting* and *watching* for His appearing will be translated. The carnal believers who are left behind will enter the day of the Lord to be chastened and purified at which time *"the saints will be raptured in groups during the tribulation as they are prepared to go."*[8]

Advocates of this viewpoint rely heavily upon the four gospels to support this interpretation. This should immediately throw up red flags in the mind of the reader inasmuch as the Body of Christ was not even in existence when our Lord carried on His earthly ministry. Partial rapturists often appeal to Luke 21:36 in support of this position. "Watch ye therefore, and pray always, that ye may be accounted worthy to escape all these things that shall come to pass, and to stand before the Son of Man." Of course, Israel is the subject of this passage; specifically, those Israelites who will be living during the time of

---

7. J. Dwight Pentecost, *Things to Come,* Pg. 165.
8. Ira E. David, *Translation: When Does It Occur? The Dawn,* Pg. 358.

Jacob's trouble. Since they are already in the day of the Lord, the *escape* is obviously not from the tribulation but from the *snare* which comes upon ". . . all them that dwell on the face of the whole earth" (Vs. 35). Thus, those who are faithful and watching are promised deliverance in that day as foretold in the Lord's prayer:

> "Our Father which art in heaven, Hallowed be Thy name. Thy kingdom come [hope]. Thy will be done in earth, as it is in heaven. Give us this day our daily bread [God will nourish them when they can no longer buy or sell]. And forgive us our debts, as we forgive our debtors. And lead us not into temptation, but deliver us from evil [i.e. the *evil one*—Antichrist]. For thine is the kingdom, and the power, and the glory, forever. Amen" (Matt. 6:9-13).

The partial rapturist by dividing the Church into two groups denies the unity of the Body of Christ (I Cor. 12:13). It also calls into question the value of the death of Christ if one group is worthy for heaven while the other group must earn their acceptance. Surely, we are all unworthy, but thanks be unto God that those who have believed the gospel are accepted in the Beloved (Eph. 1:6).

THE PRETRIBULATIONAL RAPTURE VINDICATED

We purposely have not gone into an extensive, critical analysis of the foregoing theories for this reason: When God made known the Mystery, which had been *hidden* from ages and generations past, it added an entirely *new dimension* to eschatology or "things to come." During this present age of Grace, God is doing something new and different among the *Gentiles*. However, once His plans and purposes for this administration are completed, He will

30

close this age by *catching away* the Body of Christ to heaven. This event must *precede* the tribulation in view of the fact that God's Prophetic program stands in direct contradiction with the Mystery revealed to the Apostle Paul (Col. 1:24-27). Since God is not the author of confusion, whatsoever God has *separated* let no man join together!

So then, the pretribulational Rapture position is *vindicated* on the basis of a proper understanding of the two programs of God.[9] Those who hold to *midtribulationism, prewrath rapture, posttribulationism* or *partial rapturism* expose their lack of knowledge of this very basic distinction.

Perhaps one of the strongest arguments for the translation of the Church before the tribulation is the *undeniable* fact that the Rapture is *exclusively* taught in Paul's epistles. Diligent students of the Word understand that God's prophetic clock abruptly stopped at the stoning of Stephen, which marked the fall of Israel, thus temporarily suspending the kingdom program.[10] A short time ago, a friend sent us an insightful illustration in this regard: "I was explaining to some friends that this was similar to what happens in a football game. The referee blows a whistle and the clock stops. Of course, regular time goes on but the game does not start until play resumes on the field. In just this way, God has stopped the *Prophetic clock* regarding His dealings with the nation Israel. One day that clock will start again and God will complete His program and fulfill all the promises to His chosen people."

---

9. The author's book *Exploring the Unsearchable Riches of Christ* goes into this subject more comprehensively—see page 25.

10. The stoning of Stephen was the fulfillment of Luke 19:14.

DANIEL'S 70 WEEKS (OF YEARS) IN LIGHT OF PROPHECY

490 YEARS
ONE WEEK = 7 YEARS
STONING OF STEPHEN

7 weeks or 49 years
Rebuilding of
Temple in Jerusalem
during troublous times

62 weeks or
434 years
Until the cutting
off of Messiah

1 week or 7 years
The Tribulation period
(Time of Jacob's
Trouble)

69 weeks
fulfilled

490 years

1 week
unfulfilled

The Literal
Establishment
of the 1000 year
Kingdom on earth

DANIEL'S 70 WEEKS (OF YEARS) IN LIGHT OF THE MYSTERY

STONING OF STEPHEN   **RAPTURE**

7 weeks or 49 years
Rebuilding of
Temple in Jerusalem
during troublous times

62 weeks or
434 years
Until the cutting
off of Messiah

Mystery Program
The Parenthetical
Age of Grace
(Heavenly Hope)
Nearly
2000 years

Tribulation period
(Time of Jacob's
Trouble)

69 weeks
fulfilled

1 week
unfulfilled
7 years

1 week
unfulfilled
7 years

K I N G D O M

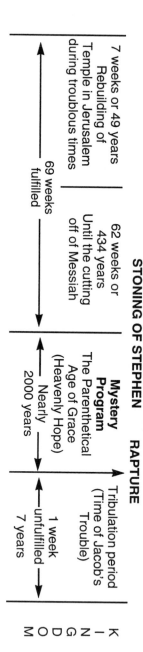

This helps to explain why Daniel's 70th week has not yet been fulfilled in prophecy. Daniel predicted that when the Messiah was cut off (at the stoning of Stephen) there would only remain one week, or seven years, of tribulation before the Second Coming and subsequent establishment of the millennial kingdom (Dan. 9:20-27). What reasonable explanation could possibly be given for Daniel's final week being left unfulfilled? The answer is really quite simple when we consider the chart on the foregoing page.

The sequence of this chart shows that the parenthetical age of Grace has temporarily *interrupted* Daniel's seventieth week. Subsequently, the Prophetic program will remain dormant until God reactivates it upon the completion of His plans and purposes for the administration of Grace. This exegesis allows us to take a *literal* interpretation of the Scriptures and eliminates the need to spiritualize Daniel's prophecy, as the posttribulationists are prone to do.

Like a summer storm when the skies begin to look threatening, there are many in our day who have observed the ominous conditions of our times. Those who have been waiting for the Lord's coming for His own are becoming increasingly uneasy that they may go through at least some part of the tribulation. This present paranoia, at least in part, has been generated by the mass media which has brought us to a higher level of awareness of world events. Global conflicts, economic earthquakes, natural disasters and terrorism around the world have caused many Christians to brace themselves, as it were, for the day of calamity. Be that as it may, it is extremely dangerous to interpret the Scriptures by *current events.* Many who have committed this error in the past have lived to regret it. During World War II, many believed

Hitler was the Antichrist, only to have to apologetically retract their statement years later.

Today is *man's* day. Therefore, the tumultuous times we are presently experiencing are the aftermath of man's sin. Furthermore, we must not forget that the powers of darkness are working feverishly behind the scenes. They are attempting to bring about a spirit of lawlessness, which eventually will usher in the tribulation period described as the *day of God's wrath* in Revelation 6, 8,9,16,19. Thankfully, the Body of Christ will never experience those things that are predicted in the Book of Revelation, for we have been *delivered* from the wrath to come (I Thes. 1:10; 5:9).

While prophecy is not being fulfilled today, the stage for the future tribulation is unquestionably being set behind the scenes. Satan, who has power over the kingdoms of this world system (Luke 4:5,6), is preparing the inhabitants of the earth for the introduction of the Antichrist. He is subtly guiding the human race toward a one-world government and a one-world religious system, which the man of sin will eventually control.

Unbeknown to many, Satan is gradually moving all the props into place as the chief actors prepare to take their places on the world's stage. Picture it something like this: Soon God will raise the curtain, which we will liken to the Rapture, then the drama of the tribulation will begin. Woe unto the inhabitants of the earth for God will *"speak unto them in His wrath, and vex them in His sore displeasure"* (Psa. 2:5). It is our prayer to God that the Holy Spirit will touch the heart of every unsaved reader to "flee from the wrath to come" by trusting Christ as their personal Savior.

34

2

Scriptural Fortification for a Pretribulational Rapture

"When Christ, who is our life, shall appear, then shall ye also appear with Him in glory."

—*Colossians 3:4*

THE PRETRIBULATIONAL RAPTURE IN I THESSALONIANS 5

An old country preacher in Indiana, teaching on the *Lord's coming,* said to his congregation one morning: "Brethren, it's a good thing we are going to be changed in a moment, in the twinkling of an eye, otherwise, there would be a riot on the way up!" Anyone who has ever defended our Lord's imminent return knows that this subject usually produces more heat than light. Thus, it is essential that we use the *Sword of the Spirit* effectively to disarm those who oppose this truth. Perhaps the two most predominant portions of Scripture that support pretribulationism are found in the Thessalonian letters. In Paul's first letter to these saints, he makes a sharp distinction between the *day of the Lord* and the *day of Christ.*

"For yourselves know perfectly that the *day of the Lord* so cometh as a thief in the night" (I Thes. 5:2).

"Ye are all the children of light, and the children of the day [i.e. of Christ]" (I Thes. 5:5).

If we follow the apostle's train of thought closely, he assumes that the reader understands the *day of the Lord*

35

is a time of trouble, distress, desolation and darkness (Zeph. 1:14,15). It is a *prophetic season* that Paul likens to the arrival of a thief in the night. The thief comes unannounced at a time that we least expect him. Of course, his trademark is the element of *surprise*. In like manner, the day of the Lord will descend upon an unfit world that is totally *unprepared* for its arrival. "It shall come as a destruction from the Almighty. Therefore shall all hands be faint, and every man's heart shall melt: And they shall be afraid: pangs and sorrows shall take hold of them. . ." (Isa. 13:6-8).

Paul emphatically states that we are not of the night, that is, the prophetic night, nor will the members of Christ's Body ever be identified with the above period of *darkness* (I Thes. 5:5). "But ye, brethren, are NOT in *darkness*, that *that day* should overtake you as a thief" (Vs. 4). In other words, the members of the Body have been enlightened as to the certainty that we will *escape* the judgment to come. *"That day"*—the day of the Lord, will not overtake us as a thief. Why? because we are the *children of the day* (Vs. 5). "Being confident of this very thing, that He which hath begun a good work in you will perform it until the *day of Jesus Christ*" (Phil. 1:6).

The phrase, *day of Christ,* is unique to Paul's revelation. It pertains to the time of the *Rapture* and subsequent *Judgment Seat of Christ* when the members of His Body will be rewarded for their faithfulness. This corroborates that the *translation of the Church* will *predate* the future tribulation. Little wonder the apostle says, "But of the times and seasons, brethren, ye have NO need that I write unto you. For yourselves know *perfectly* that the day of the Lord so cometh as a thief in the night" (I Thes. 5:1,2).

THE PRETRIBULATIONAL RAPTURE
IN II THESSALONIANS 2

Paul's second letter to those at Thessalonica is perhaps the most comprehensive affirmation made by the apostle for a pretribulational Rapture. Unfortunately, this sacred truth has been somewhat obscured by the translation of the text. So as not to be misunderstood, the author has always been a avid supporter and defender of the *King James Version*. It is our conviction that the KJV is a remarkably faithful translation of the original languages. In our opinion it stands head and shoulders above the more modern versions which are a product of inferior manuscripts. When a group of translators undertake a noble task, such as translating the Scriptures, their beliefs and theology naturally generate numerous variations. Interestingly, the KJV translators, to their credit, knew that they were handling the Word of God. Thus, they themselves humbly confessed to their fallibility and limitations. In their letters to the King and to the people, they acknowledged that the translation they produced was by no means perfect. Consider also what they had to say in the *Preface to the Reader* about the marginal notes they placed in the original 1611 Version:

"Some peradventure would have no variety of the senses in the margin, lest the authority of the Scriptures for deciding by that show of uncertainty should somewhat be shaken, but we hold their judgment not to be sound in this point. . . .they that are wise had rather their judgments at liberty in differences of readings, than to be captivated to one, when it may be the other."

Bearing these thoughts in mind, we shall now proceed

37

to give a thorough exposition of the first three verses of II Thessalonians Chapter 2:

> "Now we beseech you, brethren, by the coming of our Lord Jesus Christ, and by our gathering together unto Him" (II Thes. 2:1).

This particular passage beautifully develops the theme for the passages that follow, which clearly is the *coming* of our Lord Jesus Christ. But there are *two* comings taught in the Scriptures; therefore, it will be essential for us to establish which return of Christ is being discussed in this context.

To help us make this determination, we want to observe closely how the pronouns are used in this passage, *"Now we beseech you."* Carefully note that the apostle uses the pronoun "we" in the *representative* sense when making a reference to himself, Silas and Timothy (II Thes. 1:1). Since these three veterans of the gospel were saved by grace alone as members of the Body of Christ, they shared in common the Blessed Hope. Each of them anticipated our Lord's return for His own at the *Rapture.* Paul continues, *". . . and by our gathering together unto Him."* Here he shifts his usage to the *collective* pronoun "our" indicating that *all* members of the Body of Christ, himself included, will be gathered together at the sound of the trump. Therefore, we conclude that this same *hope* had been delivered to the Thessalonians, for they were also looking forward to that appearing of our great God and Savior Jesus Christ.

There is no doubt then, that the apostle is discussing the *Secret Coming of Christ* for the Church, commonly known as the Rapture. We should add that this blessed truth was one of the *first* promises the apostle committed to those at Thessalonica. Because there were those who were determined to rob them of this hope, Paul calls upon these dear saints to remember what he had taught them when he was yet with them (II Thes. 2:5). This should be a solemn warning to every child of God that to be drawn away from the Apostle Paul's message is to bring discord among the brethren.

> "That ye be not soon shaken in mind, or be troubled, neither by spirit, nor by word, nor by letter as from us, as that the day of Christ [the Lord] is at hand" (II Thes. 2:2).

Apparently, there arose false teachers in that day who were instructing the believers at Thessalonica that they were in the day of the Lord. Here in Verse 2 the *Authorized Version* reads "day of Christ." However, *numerous* Greek manuscripts read "Lord" instead of "Christ."[1]

May we remind the reader once again of the words of the King James translators, that one is wise to consider the *other* readings, especially in view of the fact that they did not understand the Mystery. There is a general consensus among the scholars (linguists) that the proper rendering should be *day of the Lord,* to which we wholeheartedly agree. More importantly, the context coincides with the manuscript evidence, which demands the phrase "day of the Lord."

Surely these false teachers who had infiltrated the church were not teaching that the day of Christ was present. For had this been the case, it would have been cause

---

1. Majority Text: Manuscripts F,G,L,P

for jubilation, not concern. Obviously, these false teachers were instructing these believers that they were in the day of the Lord. Consequently, they were *alarmed* at the thought that they were about to experience the seven-year tribulation period. Needless to say, this false teaching had a traumatic effect upon the local assembly. Paul's refutation of this heresy was swift.

Paul reveals that these saints were "shaken in mind" over this persuasion. The verb "shaken" denotes a rocking motion, such as a building rocking back and forth in an earthquake (Acts 16:26). In other words, those at Thessalonica were in a quandary between the pretribulational Rapture Paul had taught and the mid- or posttribulational view the false teachers were promoting. The church is also said to have been "troubled" by the report that they were in the tribulation, and rightfully so. The verb "troubled" means to be "frightened or to cry aloud," thus conveying the thought of a feeling of fright or *alarm*. Furthermore, the present tense here emphasizes the fact that they were in a *state* of alarm. Evidently, the controversy had a very unsettling effect upon the whole assembly. The situation had become so emotionally charged that it was necessary for the Apostle Paul to write them in an attempt to calm their fears.

This seems to be an appropriate place to ask a *crucial* question: If Paul had taught that the Body of Christ will go through the tribulation, as some claim, then why were these saints shaken in mind and troubled? They were shaken because Paul had taught them that they would NOT go through any part of it.

The apostle warns them, *"Let no man deceive you by*

40

any means. . ." (Vs. 3). *"Neither by spirit, nor by word, nor by letter as from us, as that the day of Christ [the Lord] is at hand"* (Vs. 2). The insidious teaching that these believers were in the day of the Lord was not of God, nor did it originate with His divinely appointed apostle. Consequently, anyone who came to them proclaiming that the Church of this age would suffer through the time of Jacob's trouble was either terribly misinformed or a deceiver.

The methods of deception employed by these unscrupulous men were varied. The first area in which these saints were to exercise caution was with those who claimed to be speaking by the *Spirit*. Apparently there were those in their midst who claimed to be prophets of God speaking under the direction of the Holy Spirit. In all probability Paul's admonition was as follows: If a prophet should predict that the Body of Christ will enter the day of the Lord, he is not a prophet of God, but rather a messenger of Satan!

The second deceptive means these saints were to be aware of concerned those who came unto them declaring that they had received a special *word of revelation* from God. Should someone come to them preaching that the *present distress* they were encountering was the tribulation, he was to be marked as a false teacher and to be avoided. The distress this church was experiencing at that time was due to their faithfulness in naming the name of Christ; it was not a result of the wrath of God (II Thes. 1:4-6 cf. I Cor. 7:26-32). The members of Christ's Body have been called upon to endure a number of these persecutions down through the centuries.

They are normally temporary in character and are usually the result of evil men seeking to suppress the truth. The Reformation period is a more recent example of these unspeakable atrocities. This is another solemn reminder of how dangerous it is to interpret the Scriptures by current events.

Another area where they were to be watchful was with those who sent *letters* to them. Undoubtedly, this had been the most effective tool of these deceivers. Under the disguise of Paul's signature, which they had forged, they had circulated a *spurious* letter at Thessalonica denouncing and retracting the truth of the pretribulational Rapture. The outcome, of course, was sheer pandemonium in the assembly. Paul sought to remedy this matter by assuring them he had never sent such a letter, nor would he. To safeguard against a repetition of this falsehood, the apostle initiated a *unique* salutation at the end of each of his epistles, which would indicate the authenticity of the document.

Thus we have: *"The salutation of Paul with mine own hand, which is the token in every epistle: so I write. The grace of our Lord Jesus Christ be with you all. Amen"* (II Thes. 3:17,18).

These touching words of grace written with Paul's own hand close all of his epistles, including Hebrews! Moreover, the assemblies in that day would now have a means of detecting a *counterfeit* epistle. Beware, for there are deceivers among us even at this hour, but thankfully, by God's grace, the truth of the pretribulational Rapture has been preserved in His Word.

TWO EVENTS THAT MUST PRECEDE
THE DAY OF THE LORD

"Let no man deceive you by any means: for that day shall not come, except there come a falling away [Gr. *hee apostasia*—'or the departure'] first, and that man of sin be revealed, the son of perdition" (II Thes. 2:3).

It is significant that the apostle discloses that two major events must precede the day of calamity. Few will question that the phrase, *"for that day shall not come"* is a direct reference to the day of the Lord. This is a foregone conclusion based upon the previous verses we have been considering. So then, Paul is declaring that the day of the Lord cannot come except there be a *falling away* first. This, perhaps, is the most substantial affirmation given in Paul's epistles for a pretribulational Rapture, wherein he meticulously establishes the fact that before the day of the Lord could commence there must first come a *falling away*. Generally speaking, this phrase has been interpreted to mean that in the latter days of this dispensation many shall apostatize from the faith they once embraced. Unfortunately, our translation has obscured the true meaning of what Paul was actually expressing.

When the apostle says, *"Study to show thyself approved. . ."* surely this is not to be limited only to the doctrines of the Bible. It also applies to the languages which cradle these doctrines. Sometimes we must consult the original languages to bring out the proper *sense* that was initially intended by the Holy Spirit. While minor adjustments may be necessary at times in our English translation, the Word of God remains unaltered.

Now, let's consider the noun *apostasia,* which is used by

43

the apostle here in II Thessalonians 2:3. The Greek word *apostasia* is generally defined as being a defection, revolt or apostasy. This term primarily has to do with *position;* however, it has been suggested that there is substantial evidence this term also has a secondary meaning, which is not uncommon in any language. This same word is found in Acts 21:21 where Paul is said to have taught the Jews ". . . *to forsake* [Gr. *apostasia] Moses. . . .*" To forsake Moses and submit to the gospel of grace implies that they had *departed* from Moses' teaching.

Turning to Joshua 22:22 we have an older form of the noun "apostasia" found in the Septuagint. *"The Lord God of gods . . . He [God] knoweth . . . if it be in rebellion [apostasis] or if in transgression against the Lord."* When the Rubenites and Gadites sinned against God by building an altar beside the Lord's altar, it was seen as an act of rebellion. To rebel against God is another way of saying they *departed* from His ways.

Since the noun receives its *root meaning* from the verb, it will be helpful to determine how the verb form of *apostasia* is used in the Scriptures. Consider these two examples: According to Acts 12:10, after the angel of the Lord brought Peter to the gate that led to the city ". . . the angel *departed* [verb form of apostasia] from him." In Acts 15:39 we read: "And the contention was so sharp between them, that they *departed* [verb form of apostasia] asunder one from the other: and so Barnabas took Mark, and sailed unto Cyprus."

There appears to be abundant evidence to translate *hee apostasia* "the departure" and we believe this is exactly the thought that Paul sought to convey. The event spoken

44

of here then by the apostle is our "departure" in the Rapture, which clearly takes place prior to the tribulation period. One of the supporting factors that substantiates this observation is a proper understanding of the fact that Paul did not receive the revelation concerning the falling away from the faith until his *later* ministry (I Tim. 4:1). But we do know that he taught the "departure" in his early ministry (I Thes. 4:13-17). Paul refreshes the Thessalonians' memory of these things with the words, *"Remember ye not, that when I was yet with you, I told you these things?"*

This writer has found himself in good company in holding the position that "the departure" is the sense of II Thessalonians 2:3. Three eminent Bible teachers from the past and present speak with a unified voice on the subject:

J. Vernon McGee writes:

"There must be 'a falling away first.' Many have interpreted this to mean the apostasy, and I agree that it does refer to that. The Greek word that is here translated as 'falling away' is *apostasia.* The root word actually means 'departure or removal from'. . . . The day of the Lord cannot begin—nor the Great Tribulation Period—until the departure of the true Church has taken place."[2]

E. Schuyler English adds to the argument:

"The Greek words, translated 'a falling away,' are *hee apostasia.* . . . *Apostasia* generally carries the meaning of *defection, revolt,* or *rebellion against God.* These are the primary meanings of the word, as found in most lexicons.

---

2. *Thru The Bible,* Vol. 5, J. Vernon McGee, Pg. 413.

There is a secondary connotation in *Liddell and Scott's Greek English Lexicon,* namely: *disappearance,* or *departure.* . . . *Apostasia,* the noun, comes from the verb *aphisteemi,* which means *to remove,* or, in the casual sense, *to put away,* or to *cause to be removed.* This root verb, *aphisteemi,* is used fifteen times in the New Testament: Luke 2:27; 4:13; 8:13; 22:29; Acts 5:37,38; 12:10; 15:38; 19:9; 22:29; II Cor. 12:8; I Tim. 4:1; 6:5; II Tim. 2:19; and Heb. 3:12. . . . 'The departure' is assuredly an acceptable translation of *hee apostasia* and is, in our opinion, the proper one.

"The day of the Lord will not come, then, until the man of sin be revealed. And before he is revealed, there must be 'the departure.' Departure from what or to what? It must have been something concerning which the Thessalonians believers were informed, else the DEFINITE ARTICLE [our emphasis] would hardly have been employed, and without any qualifying description with the noun. . . . There is a departure concerning which the Thessalonians had been instructed by letter. This is not conjecture but fact: It is the Rapture of the Church, described in I Thessalonians 4:13-17."[3]

Finally, Pastor Stam in his conclusion to II Thessalonians 2 states:

1. "The word *apostasia* and its root verb *aphisteemi* do *not,* used by themselves, mean 'apostasy' and 'apostatize.' They mean 'departure' and 'depart,' nothing more.

2. "II Thes. 2:3 states in the Greek, that the day of the

---

3. *Re-Thinking the Rapture,* E. Schuyler English, Pages 67-69.

Lord will not come 'except the departure come first, and that the man of sin be revealed, the son of perdition.'

3. "The term 'the departure,' with the definite article, denotes previous reference.

4. "Paul *had* written to the Thessalonians in his previous letter about the departure of the members of Christ's Body from this earth. . ." (I Thes. 4:16,17).[4]

THE MAN OF SIN

The second prerequisite to the ushering in of the day of the Lord is the manifestation of the Antichrist. Evidently, those at Thessalonica were being taught by these messengers of Satan that the Antichrist was already in their midst. The apostle refutes this conclusion by demonstrating that the man of sin cannot be revealed until *after* our departure. Actually, the appearance of the son of perdition on the stage of the world will mark the beginning of the day of vengeance. Incidentally, down through the years, numerous world leaders were believed by some to be the man of sin. *History, however, has borne out the precise accuracy of Holy Scripture.*

The members of the Body of Christ will, thankfully, never have the "pleasure" of being introduced to the Antichrist or even know who he is for that matter! Even though there is a *possibility* that he may be among us even at this very hour, his identity remains concealed. Upon his earthly debut he will quickly become the chief actor in the political affairs of the world.

---

4. *Thessalonians,* C. R. Stam, Pg. 125.

Whatever form of evil Satan may send our way, it is comforting to know that the Rapture will be pretribulational and that we will never see one hour of the tribulation! Every day, then, is another day of grace that draws us closer and closer to the time of our exodus from this world. Therefore, we conclude that a *proper understanding* of the Mystery demands that we hold to the truth of a pretribulational Rapture of the Church. AMEN!!

3

The Two Comings of Christ

"Even as the testimony of Christ was confirmed in
you: So that ye come behind in no gift; waiting for
the coming of our Lord Jesus Christ."
—*I Corinthians 1:6,7*

The Church recently celebrated the 476th Anniversary
of the Protestant Reformation. This period in Church history gave birth to an endless stream of godly men who
risked life and limb opposing the ramparts of tradition.
By the grace of God, they exposed the fallacy of religion
and reemphasized the importance of basing one's faith solely on the Scriptures. While the Reformers are to be credited with teaching the Second Coming of Christ, it was not
until the late 1800's that the truth of the pretribulational
Rapture was recovered.

For the past century, most believers have rejoiced in the
Blessed Hope but the reclaiming of this revelation has not
been without its conscientious objectors. Covenant Theology flatly denies any notion of a Rapture and subsequently teaches that there is only one return of Christ to
be anticipated at the close of the Great Tribulation. Most
dispensationalists believe that there will be two comings
of Christ although more and more seem to be questioning
as to whether or not the Rapture will be *pretribulational*.
Since the interpretations of men have always been many
and varied on this subject, we shall allow you to be the
judge as to what the Word of God teaches on this matter.

Second Coming	Rapture
A *prophesied* event from the foundation of the world (Jude 14,15).	An *unprophesied* event kept secret from the foundation of the world (I Cor. 15:51).

THE SECOND COMING OF CHRIST

Almost everyone agrees that the Second Coming of Christ is slated to take place at the close of Daniel's seventieth week or the end of the Great Tribulation. This particular coming of our Lord is a *prophesied event*; that is, it has been foretold by the prophets since the world began. The earliest chronological reference to this glorious advent is made by Enoch who was among the first descendants from Adam.

> "And Enoch also, the seventh from Adam, prophesied of these, saying, Behold, the Lord cometh with ten thousands of His saints" (Jude 14).

This passage takes us back to the dawn of creation, indeed, to the very beginning of time as we know it. Thus, Enoch, who is said to have walked with God, was the *first* to reveal that the Lord will return to the earth in a flaming fire of vengeance to execute judgment on His enemies. Those who twist the Scriptures to their own destruction contend that Enoch's prophecy is found nowhere in the Old Testament; therefore, it would be impossible for Jude to have quoted him. Such reasoning calls into question the veracity of God's Word. Please read the passage closely again. Jude does not imply that Enoch ever *wrote* the prophecy. Rather, he *verbally spoke* "saying" these words to those of his generation as a warning of the judgment to come. The remarkable thing about this prophecy is that the Spirit of God who caused Enoch to utter it was the *same* Spirit who revealed it to Jude by direct revelation. Being led by the Holy Spirit, Jude simply recorded in written form what Enoch had spoken nearly four thousand years earlier. Surely a knowledge of these things should further strengthen our faith in the *unity* and *inspiration* of the Scriptures!

Many have inquired through the years as to the identity of these *saints* in this passage. If we keep in mind that when Enoch originally spoke these words the Body of Christ was a safely guarded secret, this means only the *prophetic saints* could be in view. So, all those who believed under the old economy, from Adam to Stephen, including the martyrs of the future tribulation, will return with Christ in His *Second Coming.* Inasmuch as the Body of Christ has a heavenly hope and calling, we will not be numbered with this company who witness firsthand the horrors of Armageddon.

Those who have spent their lives studying the canon of Holy Scripture believe that the Book of Job is the oldest book of the Bible. If this is true, and we have no reason to doubt that it is, then Job predates the Pentateuch by four centuries.[1] Interestingly, Job also predicted the Second Advent when he wrote: "For I know that my Redeemer liveth, and that He shall stand at the latter day upon the earth" (Job 19:25). The testimonies of Enoch, Job and many others bear witness that the prophetic saints not only comprehended the Lord would return to the *earth,* they likewise looked forward to it with confident expectation.

---

1. The Pentateuch is the first five books of the Bible that were written by Moses.

THE RAPTURE OF THE CHURCH

"Behold, I show you a mystery; We shall not all sleep, but we shall all be changed, In a moment, in the twinkling of an eye, at the last trump: for the trumpet shall sound, and the dead shall be raised incorruptible, and we shall be changed" (I Cor. 15:51,52).

Have you ever looked for something only to discover later that it was never there in the first place? This very thing happened to me not long ago. I had gone across town to drop off some important papers for a friend, but upon arriving in the area I was unable to locate the address. For some unknown reason those of the male species seem to have a small voice that urges us to search, search, search, it's just around the next corner! Well, after going up and down three or four streets and around the block five times, I finally swallowed my pride and stopped to ask for directions. Of course, when I asked an old-timer the whereabouts of the address, he chuckled and said, "Son, you can't get there from here." As it turned out, the street I was looking for was in two sections and the part I wanted was on the other side of town. Consequently, I was searching for something that wasn't there to begin with!

The same can be said of the doctrine of the Rapture; one can search the pages of prophecy from beginning to end only to find that the *Secret Coming of Christ* is an *unprophesied event.* If there is one word that sums up the teaching of the Rapture in the Old Testament and the Gospels, it is SILENCE! And so it should be, for the Mystery with its secret Rapture was kept *hidden* from ages and generations past—hidden, that is, in the mind of

52

God. The Mystery program is a new entity in itself. It is distinct from God's Prophetic program and will abruptly terminate at the Secret Coming of Christ. This necessitates the Rapture be *pretribulational*. To say otherwise is to bring confusion into the camp.

The author has said many times, and it bears repeating again, the Rapture and the Second Coming are *not* two stages of the same event as some have supposed. They are two distinct comings, associated with two different programs which are separated by an interval of seven years. In summary, the Second Coming of Christ was a *prophesied* event that promises the Lord's return to the *earth* at the end of Daniel's seventieth week (Zech. 14:1-4). The Rapture, on the other hand, is an *unprophesied* event that promises the appearing of the Savior in *heaven* preceding the tribulation period (I Thes. 4:16,17).

Second Coming	**Rapture**
Christ returns as Judge and King of Kings (Rev. 19:11-16).	Christ returns as the Lord of Glory (Col. 3:4).

THE SECOND COMING

In prophecy Christ is frequently referred to as a *judge* who will one day return to the earth to execute judgment upon the ungodly. Here in Revelation 1:12-18, the Apostle John gives us a sobering glimpse of the Holy One who will judge the world in righteousness.

> "And in the midst of the seven candlesticks one like unto the Son of Man, clothed with a garment down to the foot, and girt about the paps with a golden girdle" (Vs. 13).

Standing (preparing to act) in the midst of the golden lampstands John saw one *like* the Son of Man. At first glance there seemed to be some doubt in the mind of the apostle as to whom he had seen. Was it the Son of Man or was it another? John, of course, remembered the Lord as the lowly Jesus who hungered and thirsted and grew weary from His journeys. But now the apostle was seeing the Son of Man in a completely different form, a form that startled him. He beheld Him preparing to pour out His wrath upon this evil world system.

"His head and His hairs were white like wool," which suggests He will judge righteously. "And His eyes were as a flame of fire" searching out and exposing the secrets of men. Moreover, all hidden things of dishonesty will be brought to light. "And His feet like unto fine brass, as if they were burned in a furnace." Brass is normally associated with judgment in the Scriptures, therefore, when the Son of Man returns in His fury, He shall trample His enemies under foot and their blood shall run to the horse bridles (Rev. 14:14-20). Little wonder John marvelled at the appearance of the One in the midst of the lampstands, and questioned who it was—he had never witnessed such an unbelievable sight in his life!

As the signs of the end times run their course they will be followed by the appearing of the Son of Man in heaven. With lightning speed He will descend to do battle with this sinful world. John adds, "And I saw heaven open, and behold a white horse; and He that sat upon him was called Faithful and True, and in righteousness He doth JUDGE and make war. . . . And He was clothed with a vesture dipped in blood: and His name is called The Word of God" (Rev. 19:11,13). In that day men will gaze in sheer terror as the *Judge* of all the earth overwhelms them with the glory of His presence. Like the grapes that are crushed in the vat at harvest, the blood of His enemies shall stain His garment.

Some have reasoned that perhaps the "vesture dipped in blood" here is a reference to the bloodstained garments of Calvary when the Savior died for the sins of the world. We strongly disagree for this reason: The first time Christ came He did so as the Savior of mankind; however, in His Second Coming He appears in *vengeance* to *judge* and make war. Sadly, the hour of redemption will have then passed, for those who have received the mark of the beast are doomed forever.

Furthermore, the day our Savior died they stripped Him of His robe and the soldiers cast lots for it. How then could have it been stained with His blood? Nor is this to be understood in a symbolic sense. We believe Isaiah resolves the matter when he prophesied of this future day: ". . . for I [Christ] will tread them in mine anger, and trample them in my fury; and *their* blood shall be sprinkled upon my garments, and I will stain all my raiment" (Isa. 63:3). Unsaved friend, this day of calamity looms on the horizon, not to mention that "Hell yawns before you." But there is still time. There is still hope! Take Christ today while He is still your Savior, otherwise, He will soon be your Judge. Believe that Christ died for your sins and rose again and God will save you from the *wrath to come* (Rom. 5:9; I Cor. 15:1-4).

THE RAPTURE OF THE CHURCH

With the introduction of this present dispensation, our Lord is cast in a completely different role. Today, He is the *Lord of Glory*, not willing that any should perish but that all will come to a knowledge of the truth. In the dispensation of Grace, He is *seated* (a position of rest) at the right hand of the Father far above all principalities and powers. As Christ carries out His heavenly ministry today, He is also the *Head* of the Body and has promised us, through Paul's gospel, deliverance from the time of Jacob's trouble (Col. 1:18; I Thes. 5:9-11).

> "Grace be to you, and peace, from God our Father, and from the Lord Jesus Christ" (Eph. 1:2).

We would venture to say that probably most believers have read the foregoing passage or those akin to it hundreds of times. Since these passages are read over so casually, most have concluded that they are merely Paul's salutations to the churches. However, a closer evaluation discloses that this is simply not the case. Notice it is "grace and peace from God our Father," not from Paul. In other words, this is a divine *declaration* that God has made to every member of the Body of Christ that He will *withhold* His wrath until the completion of this dispensation which will close with the Rapture.

Every day is another day of God's *grace* and *peace* which is much to be thankful for. Some though may charge that we are not in touch with reality. After all, the world is coming apart at the seams as violence and evil threaten the very fiber of our existence. It is essential that we do not confuse the *day of man* with the *day of the Lord* that lies ahead. The dreadful problems of AIDS,

56

drug abuse, violence, abortion and genocide are merely the fruits of the Adamic nature. Thus, man is reaping the consequences of his own sinful behavior which, unfortunately, sometimes touch innocent victims. When the day of the Lord begins, the inhabitants of the earth will find themselves staring into the face of the *wrath of God*. God will declare war on this old world and the battle will become so intense at times that men shall say "to the mountains and rocks, fall on us, and hide us from the face of Him that sitteth on the throne, and from the wrath of the Lamb: For the great day of His wrath is come; and who shall be able to stand?" (Rev. 6:16,17).

These things should give each of us a new sense of appreciation that we are presently living under God's declaration of *grace* and *peace*. This declaration guarantees that: (1) God has reconciled the world unto Himself, therefore giving every man an opportunity to be saved. (2) During this time of amnesty, God is not imputing their trespasses to them. (3) An armistice has been signed suspending the threat of war until God completes His plans and purposes with the Body of Christ (see the opening verses in each of Paul's Gentile epistles). (4) Salvation is by grace through faith. (5) We are kept by grace. (6) We live by grace. (7) Grace shall lead us home.

The sand in the hourglass of time is steadily dwindling away. All that remains is for the *Lord of Glory* to descend into the upper atmosphere and catch us away to forever be with Him. The Rapture of the Church will be the *Triumph of His Grace* as we who are the *trophies* of His grace are seated with Christ in the heavenlies. Then shall every man receive the praise of God (I Cor. 4:5).

57

DISPENSATIONAL THEOLOGY — PREMILLENNIAL VIEW

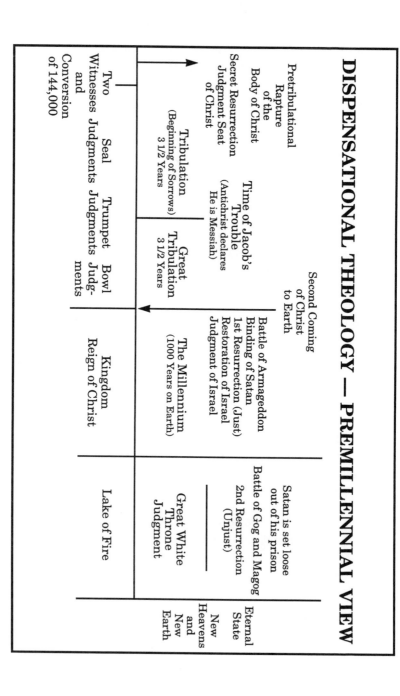

Pretribulational
Rapture
of the
Body of Christ
Secret Resurrection
Judgment Seat
of Christ

Second Coming
of Christ
to Earth

Satan is set loose
out of his prison
Battle of Gog and Magog
2nd Resurrection
(Unjust)

Tribulation
(Beginning of Sorrows)
3 1/2 Years

Time of Jacob's
Trouble
(Antichrist declares
He is Messiah)

Great
Tribulation
3 1/2 Years

Battle of Armageddon
Binding of Satan
1st Resurrection (Just)
Restoration of Israel
Judgment of Israel

The Millennium
(1000 Years on Earth)

Great White
Throne
Judgment

Eternal
State

New
Heavens
and
New
Earth

Two   Seal   Trumpet   Bowl
Witnesses Judgments Judgments Judg-
and   ments
Conversion
of 144,000

Kingdom
Reign of Christ

Lake of Fire

Second Coming	Rapture
Christ's visible return to the *earth* to redeem Israel nationally (Zech 14:4).	Christ's invisible return in *heaven* to catch away the Body of Christ (I Thes. 4:16).

THE SECOND COMING OF CHRIST

Throughout the pages of prophecy, the Second Coming of Christ is consistently depicted as taking place in full view of all the inhabitants of the earth. If you picture in your mind's eye someone parachuting into the middle of a stadium where there are 100,000 screaming fans, you have somewhat of an idea what it will be like at that day. According to the Biblical record, when all hope seems to be lost at the close of the Great Tribulation, Christ will descend from the eastern sky and *literally* stand on a well-known hill in Jerusalem.

As mentioned earlier, Job was the first to state that the Lord would stand on the *earth*. To give you some concept of the time frame we are speaking about, Job and Abraham were probably contemporaries. In both cases, wealth was determined by how many servants and cattle one possessed. Furthermore, they were both family priests. During these early days of man's existence, Job wrote: "For I know that my Redeemer liveth, and that He shall stand at the latter day upon the *earth:* And though after my skin worms destroy this body [his natural body], yet in my flesh [his resurrected body] shall I see God" (Job 19:25,26). Here in Job's journal of affliction, he found comfort in the Word of God despite all of his adversities. Graciously, God had given Job *hope* which enabled him to endure the loss of his family, all of his possessions and even his

health. He counted his eternal inheritance more important than anything this world had to offer. This is a lesson that many would do well to heed today. Perhaps it
will be helpful if we examine this promise more carefully.

"For I know that my Redeemer liveth. . . ." Undoubtedly,
Job had received his knowledge of a coming Redeemer by
direct revelation. His use of the personal pronoun "my"
indicates that he claimed God as his *personal* Redeemer,
whom we now know to be the person of Christ (Matt.
24:30 cf. Luke 21:28). The patriarch goes on to add ". . .
that He shall stand at the latter day upon the earth." Here
we are told *when* this glorious event will take place. The
latter day of prophecy is clearly a reference to the great
and terrible day of the Lord. So then, Job expected to be
raised at that day and actually see with his own eyes the
Lord return in power and glory.

Zechariah tells us the precise location on the earth
where the Messiah will stand. "And His feet shall stand
in that day upon the Mount of Olives, which is before
Jerusalem on the east, and the Mount of Olives shall
cleave in the midst thereof toward the east and toward the
west, and there shall be a very great valley; and half of
the mountain shall remove toward the north, and half of it
toward the south" (Zech. 14:4).

You will remember that at the close of our Lord's post-
resurrection ministry He ascended into heaven in plain
view of the disciples. As they stood there in wonderment
with their mouths hanging open, two angels stood by
them in white apparel and said, "Why stand ye gazing up
into heaven?" (Acts 1:11). And where were the disciples
standing at the time? "Then returned they unto Jerusalem from the MOUNT CALLED OLIVET."

So, Christ will return in His Second Coming to the exact spot that He ascended from on the Mount of Olives just prior to the day of Pentecost. Let's pause here for a moment to ponder some of the outstanding characteristics of the ascension: (1) The Lord was lifted up from the earth as a demonstration of His almighty *power*, (2) He left by way of the *east*, (3) the disciples *visibly* watched Him go, (4) angels were present, and (5) there was a manifestation of His glory as a cloud received Him out of their sight. By comparison, the Son of Man shall return in similar fashion. The angels who were present that notable day expressed it eloquently when they stated, ". . . this same Jesus, which is taken up from you into heaven, *shall so come in like manner as ye have seen Him go. . .*" (Acts 1:11 cf. Matt. 24:27-31).

Interestingly, there will be one major difference when the Lord returns to Jerusalem in the future. When the soles of His feet touch the Mount of Olives, it shall cleave to the east and to the west creating a *great valley*. Probably, this is the Valley of Jehoshaphat spoken of by the Prophet Joel. Since Jehoshaphat means "Jehovah judges" this is presumably the location where the Messiah will gather the nations to be judged (Joel 3:2 cf. Matt. 25:31-46). The reader should take great care here not to confuse the *judgment of the nations* with the *White Throne Judgment* at the end of the millennial kingdom.

THE RAPTURE OF THE CHURCH

"For the Lord Himself shall descend from heaven with a shout.... Then we which are alive and remain shall be caught up...to meet the Lord in the air..." (I Thes. 4:16,17).

61

When the trump sounds, the Body of Christ is said to be caught up into heaven at the Rapture. At this coming, the Lord remains in heaven which necessitates that we be *removed* from the earth and translated into glory. But where is heaven?

Astronomers tell us that the center of our solar system is the sun. From the standpoint of the physical universe, they are correct, of course, since the planets all orbit around the sun. According to the determinate counsel of God, however, the *earth* is the center of all God's plans and purposes (Psa. 104:5-31). Therefore, the heavens are *always* spoken of in relation to the earth, not the sun.

Of course, the theories of how many heavens are taught in the Word of God range from one to twelve. We believe that all of the references to heaven found in the Scriptures fall into one of three categories: The *first heaven* is our atmosphere where we live and move and have our being. Insofar as the heavens encompass the earth, if I were to leave from O'Hare International Airport and fly around the world at 35,000 feet, I would have never left the first heaven. The *second heaven* is our galactic system where an innumerable host of stars take us to the outer reaches of the known universe (Gen. 1:14-18). The *third heaven* is the heaven of heavens or the abode of God which brings us to a place beyond the realm of time (Deut. 10:14 cf. Psa. 2:4).

In I Corinthians 9:26, Paul emphasizes that his efforts in proclaiming the gospel were not like the Isthmian fighter who merely "beateth the *air.*" The term "air" in this passage, without question, signifies our atmosphere. It is the same word found in I Thessalonians 4:17 where we are said to be translated ". . . to meet the Lord in the air." Thus, the Lord is going to descend into the region of the first heaven, then both the dead in Christ and we who are alive and remain will be caught up together to meet Him in the upper atmosphere. Since this is a planned meeting, many have concluded that this may also be where the Judgment Seat of Christ will occur.

Unlike the Second Advent, the "Lord's coming in the air" will not be visible to the inhabitants of the earth (I Cor. 15:51,52). One reason for this is "we shall all be changed, in a moment, in the twinkling of an eye." E. W. Vine describes a "moment" as an increment of time which is indivisible. Thus, the velocity of our change will be so sudden that we shall be translated to glory in an instant. The day following the Rapture, the headlines of the world's newspapers will probably read, "Entire Christian Community Vanishes—Hallelujah!"

Because the Savior will remain hidden away in heaven, not one eye shall see Him nor shall the graves be opened, which is in keeping with the nature of our program. Inasmuch as all these events transpire simultaneously, it is possible that the sounding of the trumpet may serve a twofold purpose. It will break the silence of this dispensation, bringing it abruptly to a close, and mark the ominous beginning of the tribulation period.

Second Coming	Rapture
Judgment of Israel and the nations on earth (Matt. 25:31).	The Judgment Seat of Christ in heaven (II Cor. 5:10).

THE SECOND COMING

The purpose of the Second Coming is to deliver Israel from the hand of her oppressors and establish the millennial kingdom. But before anyone is permitted entrance into the kingdom, Christ will judge Israel and the nations. After the angels regather Israel back into the Promised Land, the Judge of all the earth will cause her to pass under the *rod* (Ezk. 20:33-40). In Biblical times, the shepherd made the sheep pass under the rod for three reasons: (1) to number the flock, (2) segregate the sick and injured, and (3) separate those that were not his possession.

This is a striking picture of what will transpire when Christ establishes the throne of His glory in Jerusalem. The Great Shepherd will cause the entire sheepfold to pass under His divine scrutiny. Those children of the devil who were rebels and rejected their Messiah will be separated from the fold and cast into outer darkness. Believing Israel will inherit the blessings of the kingdom promised to her *from* the foundation of the world (Matt. 13:36-43). Those of this number who suffer afflictions will have the Great Physician attend to their infirmities, for there is *healing in His wings* (Isa. 35:1-10 cf. Mal. 4:2). Moreover, when the numbering of the flock is completed only believers will be permitted access into the *golden age.*

Israel's review is immediately followed by the *judgment of the nations* recorded for us in Matthew 25:31-43. They, too, must pass under the rod of the King. "And before Him shall be gathered all nations: and He shall separate them one from another, as a shepherd divideth his sheep from the goats: And He shall set the sheep on His right hand,

64

but the goats on the left" (Vs. 32,33). The *sheep* in this context are those individuals who treated Israel favorably during the time of Jacob's trouble. These are the righteous from among the nations who fed, clothed and housed God's chosen ones in their hour of trial. Subsequently, the Gentiles will also enjoy many blessings of the kingdom, although the very order of these judgments suggest they will not have the rights and privileges afforded the elect nation. We might add that these are the "other sheep" in John 10:16 which will be joined to the righteous in Israel to make one fold and one Shepherd. Perhaps we should pause here momentarily to give an additional comment on this since it has been such a stumbling block in the minds of many.

> "And other sheep I have, which are not of this fold: them also I must bring, and they shall hear my voice; and there shall be one fold, and one Shepherd" (John 10:16).

Those who are Acts 2 dispensationalists normally hold the position that the ones who "are not of this fold" are the members of the Body of Christ. This is an inexcusable dispensational blunder, but it is understandable since they do not consistently rightly divide the Word of truth. Once again, we must ask ourselves the question: To whom was our Lord speaking, and at what time? The discourse on the Good Shepherd was delivered by Christ when He was on the earth at least *two years* before the Apostle Paul was given his *special revelation.* Insofar as Paul was the *first* to receive the truth of the *One Body,* the "other sheep" in the above context could in no way be the Body of Christ.

But there's more. None of the Apostle Paul's *Gentile epistles* contain a reference to the members of Christ's Body being sheep, much less a sheepfold. However, these metaphors are found throughout the pages of prophecy, which serves as another distinguishing factor between the two programs of God.

> "Behold, the days come, saith the Lord, that I will make a new covenant with the house of Israel, and with the house of Judah" (Jer. 31:31).

Under the reign of Rehoboam, the kingdom was divided in Israel. The division proved to be devastating as the ten northern tribes, which came to be called the *house of Israel,* appointed Jeroboam as their King.[2] He, of course, destroyed the religious unity of the nation when he erected altars at Dan and Bethel and caused the children of Israel to offer sacrifices unto the gods of Egypt (I Kings 12:16-31).

On the other hand, the *house of Judah* (tribes of Judah and Benjamin) followed in the ways of the Lord and continued to offer their sacrifices in *Jerusalem,* thus obeying the Law and the prophets. They remained in the Lord's *favor* in spite of the fact that He allowed them to be carried off into the Babylonian captivity for their lapse of faith. These two tribes were by far the more spiritual tribes in Israel, not to mention that it was in Bethlehem of *Judaea* where the Prince of Peace chose to be born.

Consequently, some believe that the "other sheep" are the ten northern tribes who will be brought back into the

---

2. By the time of Christ both the northern and southern tribes came to be known as the *house of Israel* even though they were yet estranged and scattered among the nations (Matt. 15:24 cf. Acts 1:6).

fold at the Second Coming of Christ. Hence, there will be one fold and one Shepherd. We surely concur that there will be a reunification of the tribes of Israel as represented by the binding of the *two sticks* in Ezekiel 37:15-28. This, however, must not be confused with the sheepfold. Israel is the sheep of God, whether they were of the northern or southern tribes. The Lord would have never called His *chosen people* the "other sheep." They are *the sheep* and, therefore, the *primary* fold.

If we say that the ten northern tribes are the "other sheep," then what about the *kingdom Gentiles*—where do they fit into the picture? It is often overlooked, but God had made a provision in prophecy for the Gentiles to be saved *through* Israel. Thus, they are also said to be *joined* to the Lord. And Isaiah goes on to add, "Even them [the Gentiles] will I bring to my holy mountain, and make them joyful in my house of prayer. . ." (Isa. 56:6,7). Insofar as the Gentiles are the last *non-Jewish converts* to be reached under the Great Commission, the classification "other sheep" fits them perfectly. But some are sure to inquire: "Are the Gentiles ever called *sheep* in prophecy?" Indeed they are; please read prayerfully Matthew 25:31-46.

Figuratively, the "goats" in this passage (Matthew 25:31-46) speak of the *unregenerate* who add additional misery to Israel's plight. An illustration of the "goat's" close association with *sin* in the Scripture is found in the story of Joseph. You will recall how Joseph's brethren killed a young goat and dipped his coat of many colors in its blood to cover up their *sin*. Thus, those from among the nations who are found in their sins, represented here as goats, will be separated from the righteous.

67

Condemned for their unbelief and cruel treatment of the children of God, the Son of Man will be left with no other recourse than to declare: "Depart from me, ye cursed [the goats on His left hand], into everlasting fire, prepared for the devil and his angels" (Matt. 25:41).

THE RAPTURE OF THE CHURCH

One of the distinct features of the Secret Coming of Christ is that our judgment is going to take place in *heaven*. God has predetermined the hour of this judgment as set forth in I Thessalonians 4:17.

> "Then we which are alive and remain shall be caught up together with them in the clouds, to MEET the Lord in the air."

The term "meet" used here by the apostle collects our thoughts around the idea of a *"planned meeting."* If you run into a friend on the street, that's a chance meeting. If your friend invites you over for dinner, that would be a *planned* meeting. This latter usage is the sense of the word used by Paul; so, the Body of Christ has an appointment with destiny that was prearranged *before* the foundation of the world (Rom. 14:10 cf. Eph. 1:4,5).

Unlike the judgments in the kingdom, only *believers* who are members of the Body of Christ in particular will appear at the Judgment Seat of Christ. Sins are not the issue at the Bema Seat for we have already been washed in the blood. But there will be a thorough examination of our *conduct* from the time of conversion.

The Federal Reserve is the regulatory branch of the government that oversees all lending institutions. They have the right to request an accounting of banking procedures and audit any or all accounts at their discretion. Any hint of impropriety can bring a swift reprimand or even demotion. If this is true in the affairs of men, how much more so in the affairs of God. The Lord of Glory is going to require an *accounting* at the hand of every member of the Body of Christ. Every thought, action, deed and even our motives will be reviewed at the Judgment Seat of Christ to determine how faithful we were to the cause of Christ.

After our reigning position is determined at the Bema Seat, we shall be seated with Christ in the heavenlies far above all principalities and powers. As Gentiles, we are citizens of heaven—trophies of His grace. First class citizens, that is, who have rights and privileges as the sons of God. Think of it, we shall reign with Christ in glory, honor and power for eternity!

A SUPPLEMENTARY THOUGHT

The words of the great hymn writer, John Peterson, seem appropriate at this point:

"Coming again, coming again; may-be morning, may-be noon; may-be evening; may-be soon!

"Coming again, coming again; O what a wonderful day it will be—Jesus is coming again!"

Thankfully, "Jesus is coming again," but it is very important to distinguish between His coming for the Body of Christ preceding the tribulation and His Second Coming following it. This can only be accomplished, however, by having a proper knowledge of what Paul calls the *Mystery*.

4

The Last Days

"Now the Spirit speaketh expressly, that in the latter times some shall depart from the faith, giving heed to seducing spirits, and doctrines of devils."

—*I Timothy 4:1*

Throughout the generations, mankind has been enthralled with *future* events. Today, the forecasting of "things to come" is a multi-million dollar business. In fact, there are those in this country who would not even dare to begin their day without first consulting their *horoscope.* Though the future might be an area of fascination, it is also one of grave danger. History is riddled with the broken promises of those who claimed to *see through time.*

The 16th century French astrologer and physician Nostradamus is said to have made over 1,000 predictions about the future which are recorded in quatrains. Historians have marveled at the accuracy of many of his predictions. He foretold, for example, the revolution in France, the rise of Napoleon and the establishment of the Royal Family in England. Yet, many of his so-called prophecies are inaccurate while others remain unfulfilled. Biblicists have also noted that many of his quatrains directly *contradict* the Scriptures concerning "things to come." Of course, the devices of Satan are many, and even though Nostradamus may have sought to predict the future, he could not have been a prophet of God by Old

71

Testament standards. In time past, the prophets had to be one hundred percent *accurate*, one hundred percent of the time! Anything short of this meant death by stoning (Deut. 18:20-22). But more importantly, the office of the prophet has been temporarily abandoned during the administration of Grace (I Cor. 13:8).

The Scriptures are the only record sanctioned by God that give us insight on what lies ahead. Thus, if we are to understand anything about the future, we must consult the written Word of God! Those who do otherwise intrude into those things which they know nothing about, vainly puffed up by their fleshly minds (Col. 2:18).

As a boy growing up in the late forties and early fifties, life seemed far more tranquil than the evil days in which we are now living. Radio was our main contact with the outside world and aside from *Sputnik* streaking across the nighttime sky things were fairly uneventful. On the home front, a major crisis amounted to someone getting their windows soaped in the neighborhood or a baseball sailing through Mrs. Sheaffer's picture window. In those bygone days of innocence, it would have been difficult to comprehend how those things recorded in the Book of Revelation could possibly come to pass.

How things have changed, and sad to say not for the better. Today, the world revels in its wicked ways and has a total disregard for righteousness. Most nations are on the verge of economic collapse while others are engaged in destroying one another. The *New World Order* that we hear so much about is simply another step toward the future one-world government and monetary system of the Antichrist. Never before in the history of mankind have

72

world affairs been so closely aligned with the coming events of the day of the Lord. It is only a matter of time until God unleashes His wrath upon this evil world system. *Of course, as the tribulation draws nearer, so does the Rapture which must precede it.* Consequently, it is essential to carefully distinguish between the *last days* of prophecy and the *last days* of this present dispensation.

THE LAST DAYS IN RELATION TO PROPHECY AND THE MYSTERY

The Old Testament prophets give us a great deal of insight into the last days of prophecy, commonly known as the Great Tribulation (Isa. 2:2-19; Joel 2:25,26). These ominous times that lay ahead are directly associated with *signs, times* and *seasons.* A sign is "a mark, indication or token and is used of that which distinguished a person or thing from others . . . as a warning or admonition." Numerous *signs* will precede the Second Coming of Christ, leaving no doubt that one of the most monumental events in history will soon take place. Who will be able to dismiss the warning of the heavens when the sun is turned into darkness and the moon into blood? Were it not for a brief delay between the *signs* at the end of the Great Tribulation and the *sign of His coming,* the Lord's return could probably be narrowed down to the day (Matt. 24:29, 30). The last days of prophecy are indisputably identified with a divine exhibition of *miraculous* signs and wonders that will be witnessed by all the inhabitants of the earth.

The above must never be confused with the *last days* taught in the Pauline epistles. Since this period concerns the Body of Christ, we must confine our study to Paul's writings where we learn that *trends,* not signs, will be prevalent as the age of Grace draws to a close. A *trend* is defined as "a current style or preference . . . the general movement in the course of time of a statistically detectable change." The key phrase here is "in the course of time." This indicates that trends tend to emerge gradually over a period of months or years and then slowly fade from the scene. For example, in the fifties the popular hairstyle for men was the *crew cut* or a *flat top*. This all changed in the sixties as *long hair* became the order of the day; so much so that it was difficult to tell the difference between men and women. The seventies and eighties brought us the *wild, let-it-be look,* and presently the *neat look* is in vogue which is something, indeed, to be thankful for! The point is that none of these hairstyles appeared overnight, although it could be correctly said that they evolved over a span of time until they became widely accepted.

Similarly, the *trends* that Paul outlines for us in II Timothy 3:1-12 will also emerge over a period of years and gradually intensify to the degree that everyone will come under their realm of influence. So then, certain *trends* will manifest themselves as we enter the last days of the administration of Grace while we await the Lord's coming in the air.

PAUL'S LAST DAYS

"This know also, that in the last days perilous times shall come" (II Timothy 3:1).

Paul warns all those in Christ Jesus that in the last days perilous times shall come. Many have taken this warning lightly, but God would have us *prepare* ourselves to avoid becoming a spiritual casualty due to a lack of

74

preparation. If we were engaged in a military operation, it would be important to gather as much intelligence on the enemy as possible. The size of the unit, how heavily armed and how well they are supplied must be determined before the conflict begins. As the last days loom on the horizon, now is the time to gather spiritual intelligence to *prepare* ourselves for those sinister times ahead. The apostle says, "This know also...." What do we need to know? What should we expect to face?

First of all, "perilous times shall come." In Matthew 8:28 the term "perilous" is translated "exceeding fierce" when referring to Legion who was possessed of many devils (See Luke 8:30). Thus, the last days are characterized as being *exceedingly* fierce wherein evil men will wax worse and worse. Whatever we may be called upon to endure at the hands of men will be nothing compared to the wrath of God in the coming day of the Lord. As Paul describes some of the characteristics accompanying the last days in verses 2-4, it could be said that these dispositions have troubled every generation to some degree. This is true, of course; however, the apostle infers that these *trends* will intensify to epidemic proportions resulting in the near collapse of morality and authority.

1. Characteristics of Men

"For men shall be lovers of their own selves, covetous, boasters, proud, blasphemers, disobedient to parents, unthankful, unholy, without natural affection, trucebreakers, false accusers, incontinent, fierce, despisers of those that are good, traitors, heady, highminded, lovers of pleasures more than lovers of God" (II Tim. 3:2-4).

If we did not know better, this almost sounds like an article out of this morning's newspaper! Paul is describing for us the *moral* and *spiritual condition* of the world preceding the Rapture of the Body of Christ. It is not our intent to enter into an exhaustive discussion of the trends set forth here by the apostle. We propose simply to comment briefly on three of these characteristics, so the reader will be in a better position to capture the sense of Paul's words.

"For men shall be lovers of their own selves. . . ." As we approach the consummation of this age, men will become more and more *self-centered.* A case in point is the present day teaching of *self-love, self-esteem* and *self-worth.* The influence of this unsound doctrine has nearly permeated every strata of Christendom. Like the beat of a drum, this theme is heard almost constantly from the pulpits of America and frequently appears on the pages of Christian literature. Beware when you hear or read: "It is important to feel good about *yourself,"* "Learn to love *yourself,"* "Probe *your* innermost self to understand why *you* think and feel as *you do,"* "God sent His Son to die for you because *you* are of great value." Satan never rests in his insatiable desire to corrupt the Word of God.

On the surface these phrases may seem commendable, but in reality they are diametrically opposed to the Scriptures. The above has been weighed in the balance and found to be wanting. For example: "The heart [innermost self] is deceitful above all things, and desperately wicked: who can know it?" (Jer. 17:9). Paul concurred when he said, "For I know that in me (that is, in my flesh, [old nature or self]) dwelleth no good thing. . ." (Rom. 7:18).

76

The old man (self) is at *enmity* against God. He hates God and the things of God and left to himself he will not seek God. The Scriptures, from beginning to end, speak with a unified voice that the *old nature* is rotten to the core (See Rom. 3:9-18).

Consequently, our old man (self) has been crucified with Christ. Paul made reference to this when he wrote to the Galatians, "I am crucified with Christ [i.e. his old man]: nevertheless I live [Paul's new nature]; yet NOT I [self], but Christ liveth in me. . . ." We are to *put off* the old nature and *put on* the new, which is created in holiness and righteousness (Eph. 4:22-24). It is futile to improve one's self-image, especially since God abhors any attempt to do so. Rather, we are to conform ourselves to the *image* of His dear Son. Thus, those of the household of faith are to live accordingly:

> "Let nothing be done through strife or vainglory; but in lowliness of mind let each esteem other better than themselves. Look not every man on his own things, but every man also on the things of others. Let this mind be in you, which was also in Christ Jesus" (Phil. 2:3-5).

Self takes great pleasure in acclaim, indulgence, approval and praise. It *glories* in all these things. But are we not robbing God when self is esteemed more highly than His glory? "What? know ye not that your body is the temple of the Holy Spirit which is in you, which ye have of God, **AND YE ARE NOT YOUR OWN?** For ye are bought with a price: therefore *glorify* God in your body, and in your spirit, *which are God's*" (I Cor. 6:19,20).

Shall we permit the "love of one's self " doctrine to overshadow the love of God in Christ Jesus? God forbid! May God help us to stand against this insidious teaching that essentially robs God of the glory that is rightfully due Him.

A spirit of independence will also prevail throughout the land. I can remember a time when everything centered around the *home,* the church and the community. A new day brought the milkman or baker to the door giving everyone an opportunity to chat and share their concerns about the neighborhood. Since everyone knew one another, a walk to the corner grocery store meant stops along the way to visit with friends. Unfortunately, those days have passed and with them our involvement in the lives of others. Consequently, we have fewer opportunities to witness for Christ.

In our modern day of advanced technology, man has managed to become so self-sufficient that he has isolated himself from others. Consider this solemn thought for a moment: We drive to the service station where we pay at the pump, then stop by a cash machine to do our banking, purchase a hamburger at the drive-thru window at McDonald's and electronically open and close the garage door upon arriving at home. Whether we realize it or not, we have successfully avoided any personal contact with those around us simply for the sake of convenience.

To complicate matters further, our children are taught that man has evolved from the lower life forms, therefore denying the very existence of God. Humanism naturally follows, erecting a philosophy that man is the sum total of all things—he is the alpha and omega. The humanist claims that human wisdom has brought us to where we

78

are today; hence, it is important to get in touch with ourselves. After all, "You owe it to yourself." Little wonder the world is in the state it is! Man has become a god unto himself with no room for the true and living God or his fellow man.

"Covetous," of course, means that men will be consumed with the *love of money* which is an inescapable fact of our generation. This insatiable desire to have more and more possessions is destroying the family unit. Business as well has trodden down this path of no return. Pride in workmanship and product quality have taken a back seat to the all-consuming desire to "get rich quick."

The management of gain is observed on every hand. Everytime you enter a supermarket, the management is manipulating you through the store. Here is a case in point: Have you ever noticed that when you go into the market to purchase milk and eggs they are seldom at the front of the store? Nine times out of ten, these two items are at the back of the store, which means you must pass the soda, snacks and those irresistible sale items at the end of each aisle. Products normally priced $2.29 marked down to $.99—who could possibly resist? So a trip to the supermarket to purchase two staples ends up costing you a bundle. This has all been engineered by the store management to entice you to buy additional products which results in a handsome financial profit. It takes discipline to shop these days!

"Without natural affection. . . ." Only a short time ago, it would have been difficult to understand what form this could have possibly taken. Today, self-love and the lack of *natural affection* is seared into the conduct of our nation.

Who would have thought that we would ever see the time that a mother's love and affection for her unborn child would wax cold. Since Biblical times, conception and birth have been celebrated as joyous occasions as a new life was received as a gift from God (Gen. 21:1-8). Today, however, in many cases conception has become a curse for the child who is unwanted. Last year alone in this country, there were 1.5 million *reported* abortions performed! That's approximately 4,000 abortions per day, at an average cost of $300 to $400 each. The slaying of the innocents has become a multi-million dollar industry!

At the time of Christ's birth, King Herod decreed that in Bethlehem all infants 2 years of age and under should be slain. How many do you suppose lost their lives? At any rate, throughout history this massacre has come to be known as *the slaughter of the innocents*. Although we are horrified at Herod's insensitive crime, it pales by comparison to the abortion rate today. The mother of the unwanted child who is contemplating an abortion, along with the physicians who perform the abortions, are disgraceful examples of what it means to be *"without natural affection."*

> "God that made the world and all things therein, seeing that He is the Lord of heaven and earth, dwelleth not in temples made with hands; Neither is worshipped with men's hands, as though He needed any thing, seeing He giveth to all life, and breath, and all things" (Acts 17:24,25).

> "Behold, I [David] was shapen in iniquity; and in sin did my mother conceive me" (Psa. 51:5).

When does life begin? The sense of this passage is not

that David's mother had committed a sinful act in desiring to have a child. Instead, he declares that he was brought forth in a state of iniquity: "My mother who conceived me was sinful and I too am sinful." Note the personal pronoun *"me"*: "In sin did my mother *conceive me,"* indicating that life begins *at conception.* Biochemists tell us, "At the moment of conception there is a complete genetic package programmed for development into a mature adult. *Nothing will be added* except time and nutrition. Each stage of development, from fertilization to old age, is merely a maturing of what is *entirely* there at the start" (my emphasis).

> "For Thou didst form *my* inward parts; Thou didst weave me in my mother's womb.[1] I will praise Thee; for I am fearfully and wonderfully made: marvellous are Thy works; and that my soul knoweth right well" (Psa. 139:13,14).

God states concerning Jeremiah, "Before I formed thee in the belly I knew thee; and before thou camest forth out of the womb I sanctified thee, and I ordained thee a prophet unto the nations" (Jer. 1:5). At the very moment of conception, even before Jeremiah was fully developed in the womb, God knew him! Insofar as God is the giver of all life, He knew Jeremiah's name, character, temperament and that one day he would come to be known as the "weeping prophet." If Jeremiah's mother had had an abortion, it would have been *Jeremiah* who was killed! His mother would never have known his name or rejoiced in what God was going to accomplish through his life.

---

1. This, we believe, is the sense of the passage.

Recently, I viewed the film *The Silent Scream,* which graphically showed an actual abortion taking place from *inside the womb.* The unborn child was still in the first trimester (first 12 weeks) of the stages of development, being fully formed with eyelashes and fingernails. When the *instrument of death* was placed into the womb, you could see the little one drawing back instinctively, sensing danger. At the instant of death, there was a violent movement as the unborn child opened his mouth as to *scream* from the trauma. It was a traumatic moment for me to have witnessed an abortion *murder* actually taking place.

> "But now he [David's child] is dead, wherefore should
> I fast? Can I bring him back again? I shall go to him,
> but he shall not return to me" (II Sam. 12:23).

We need not even discuss the *end* of those who are involved in the abortion process. Suffice it to say that "It is a fearful thing to fall into the hands of the living God" (Heb. 10:31), into the hands of Him who gave us the solemn commandment: *"Thou shalt not kill"* (Ex. 20:13).

But what about the *unborn,* who have been the victims of the genocide of our modern day? My personal conviction, is that God has made a very special provision for the unborn and for infants who have not yet arrived at the age of accountability—which varies from child to child.

As we have already witnessed, the Spirit revealed to David that even at conception he was a *sinner* before God. We are all sinners who are only capable of producing sinful offspring—humanity is a dying race which produces dying children. Because the unborn have sinned in Adam they, too, are under the sentence of death. To remedy this condition, we believe God graciously intervenes on behalf

82

of children who are not yet to the age of *accountability*. Apparently, God's infinite mercy covers them as a cloak, inasmuch as they have never been able either to accept or reject the gospel. Having never committed an act of sin, their sin in Adam is washed away by the shed blood of Christ, making them fit for heaven (II Cor. 5:17). *Mark well, however, that all others are required to believe on the Lord Jesus Christ or suffer the eternal consequences* (Acts 16:31; II Thes. 1:7-9; Rev. 20:11-15).

When David lost his infant son to the "grim reaper" his words to his servants were prophetic, "I shall go to him, but he shall not return to me." These words were not spoken in the emotion of the moment, but rather under the direction of the Spirit. We find that David took comfort in the fact that when he, himself, would some day walk through the valley of the shadow of death he would once again see his son. Since we know that David was saved, it is evident that *both* he and his son will be in the eternal presence of God.

The abortion mills of our day grieve the very heart of Almighty God! The Apostle Paul teaches us, as believers, that we are to be followers or imitators of God (Eph. 5:1). In other words, we should love what He loves and hate what He hates! Abortion is an abomination in the sight of God, which means that the slaying of today's innocents should also be repulsive in the sight of every born again believer. "Lo, children are an heritage of the Lord: and the *fruit of the womb* is His reward" (Psa. 127:3).

The sanctity of life *always* has been held in high esteem by our Heavenly Father. Let us also be guardians for the preservation of life by encouraging mothers *and*

83

fathers to take more *responsibility for their actions* by protecting the lives of their unborn children. There is another alternative to abortion—ADOPTION! We need to pray that the mothers of this nation will come to their senses so that they will stop having their young killed. Pray God will save them and cause them to realize that the life within them just might be destined to greatness in the eyes of the Lord, like a Jeremiah or an Apostle Paul (Jer. 1:5; Gal. 1:15).

2. A Form of Godliness

"Having a form of godliness, but denying the power thereof: from such turn away" (II Tim. 3:5).

Man has always been inherently religious. This may take the form of the animist who worships nature or the eastern cults that worship idols and practice self-mutilation. With a growing sense of *feudalism,* in the last days the world will flock to the house of religion to fill the longing of their souls. However, multitudes will be led astray by religious leaders who merely have a *form* of godliness. They will have the *outward semblance* of godliness, but it will be nothing more than a cheap imitation of the real thing. With their lips they will honor God, but in reality their hearts shall be far from Him. Since the natural man does not want to hear that he is a sinner, these godless leaders will proclaim a *social gospel* mingled with political concerns. Their format has no place for the Deity of Christ or His finished work. Paul says they will "deny the power thereof," that is, they will reject the preaching of the Cross and dismiss the blood of Christ as repulsive. Thus, the apostle admonishes us, "FROM SUCH TURN AWAY."

84

Any pastor, teacher, missionary or ministry that questions the finished work of Christ must be avoided. "Neither is there salvation in any other: for there is none other name under heaven given among men, whereby we must be saved" (Acts 4:12). It has been rightfully said that Hell will be filled with religious men and women.

Obviously this phrase "having a form of godliness" will manifest itself in many ways. A good example may be found in the teachings of the *New Age Movement.* Norman Geisler, Professor of Theology at *Dallas Theological Seminary* writes: "At least 14 doctrines are typical of New Age religions. While not all New Age groups hold all these beliefs, most groups embrace most of them. And all groups are characterized by the pantheistic perspective reflected in them.

"These beliefs are: (1) an impersonal god (force), (2) an eternal universe, (3) an illusory nature of matter, (4) a cyclical nature of life, (5) the necessity of reincarnations, (6) the evolution of man into Godhood, (7) continuing revelations from beings beyond the world, (8) the identity of man with God, (9) the need for meditation (or other consciousness-changing techniques), (10) occult practices (astrology, mediums, etc.), (11) vegetarianism and holistic health, (12) pacifism (or anti-war activities), (13) one world (global) order, and (14) syncretism (unity of all religions)."[2]

---

2. Bibliotheca Sacra, Volume 144, January—March 1987, Number 573, *The New Age Movement* by Norman L. Geisler, Pg. 85.

Professor Geisler also exposes the basic contrast between *Biblical Christianity* and *The New Age pantheism:*

	Biblical Christianity	*New Age Pantheism*
God	Father	Force
	Personal	Impersonal
	Only Good	Good and evil
	Created all things	Is all things
Man	Made like God	Is God
	Is evil	Is good
	Spirit/body	Spirit only
	Resurrection	Reincarnation
Jesus Christ	Same Person	Different persons ("Jesus" and "Christ")
	God-Man	God Spirit in man
	Death/resurrection	Death/reincarnations
Salvation	From moral guilt	From disharmony
	By grace	By human effort
	Victory over sin	Victory over fear
Faith	In divine power	In human potential
	Objective focus	Subjèctive focus
	To see God's will done	To see man's will done
Miracle	Done at God's command	Done at man's command
	Supernatural power (of the Creator)	Supranormal power (of creatures)
	Associated with good	Associated with evil[3]

The warning is clear: BELIEVER BEWARE!!

---

3. Bibliotheca Sacra, Volume 144, January—March 1987, Number 573, *The New Age Movement* by Norman L. Geisler, Pg. 101,102.

3. Miracle Workers

"Now as Jannes and Jambres withstood Moses, so do these also resist the truth: men of corrupt minds, reprobate concerning the faith. But they shall proceed no further: for their folly shall be manifest unto all men, as their's also was" (II Tim. 3:8,9).

Prior to our Lord's return, there are going to be those who will claim to have the power to perform miracles. Paul swiftly exposes these deceivers by comparing them with Jannes and Jambres who withstood Moses in Egypt (Ex. 7:11,12). The remarkable thing about these two magicians, who stood in Pharaoh's court, was their uncanny ability to do miracles by the power of Satan. To demonstrate the mighty hand of God, Aaron cast down Moses' rod before Pharaoh and it miraculously turned into a living serpent. But, amazingly Jannes and Jambres threw down their rods and they, too, became serpents. These evildoers challenged the servants of the Most High and we can expect the end-time seducers to do the same. "But evil men and *seducers* shall wax worse and worse, deceiving, and being deceived" (Vs. 13). E. W. Vine defines the Greek word *Goes* (seducer) as one who wails. "Hence, from the howl in which spells were chanted, a wizard, sorcerer, enchanter."[4] In other words, these impostors will weave their *miraculous* manifestations on the looms of magical arts.

But what possible purpose could Satan hope to accomplish by having his ministers of darkness perform miracles in the sight of men? This will be one of the many means whereby he will *deceive* men. While Satan is inferior to God, he does possess extraordinary power to do mighty wonders (II Thes. 2:9). He afflicted Job just short of caus-

---

4. *Expository Dictionary of New Testament Words,* E. W. Vine., Pg. 252.

ing his death. One can only conclude that he also has the power to remove the affliction and heal. In Luke 4:5,6, the devil flashed all of the kingdoms of the world before the Savior in a moment of time. Furthermore, during the future tribulation he will empower the false prophet to call fire down from heaven (Rev. 13:13,14). In the last days of this dispensation, the adversary will use miracles to deceive the world and turn the hearts of men away from the living Word by enticing them to follow *experience.*

4. Three Safeguards

"But thou hast fully known my doctrine, manner of life, purpose. . ." (II Tim. 3:10).

How can the child of God avoid falling victim to the evil influences of the last days? There are *three safeguards* that if applied daily will keep us from spiritual harm. First, we must familiarize ourselves with all of the *doctrines* taught by the Apostle Paul in his epistles. Doctrine always affects our walk. If you believe the Church is going through the tribulation, then you should be storing food and water and praying that the Antichrist does not declare himself to be God on the Sabbath. However, if you hold, as we do, that Paul teaches that the Church is to be delivered from the wrath to come, then we should spend our time more wisely by leading men and women to Christ.

Second, we must follow Paul's *manner of life* even as he followed Christ. Paul loved the Lord and by the grace of God sought to apply the Word of God in every area of his life. His heart's desire was to be more like Christ—patient, humble, kind and esteeming others better than

88

himself. Finally, diligence should be taken to carry out the *purpose* that was given to the apostle. And what was Paul's purpose in the ministry? To finish his course with joy and "make all men see what is the fellowship of the Mystery" (Acts 20:24; Eph. 3:9). May God give us this *same* burden to the praise of His glory.

5. Final Trials

"Persecutions, afflictions, which came unto me at Antioch, at Iconium, at Lystra; what persecutions I endured: but out of them all the Lord delivered me" (II Tim. 3:11).

What prompted the apostle to single out these *three cities* from the others he had visited on his apostolic journeys? The answer is twofold: First, the rejection of the gospel of the grace of God greatly intensified. Second, Paul's persecutions grew increasingly worse in each of these cities. At Antioch, the enemies of the Cross *reviled* Paul and Barnabas and forced them out of the city. At Iconium, things deteriorated even further when their very *lives were threatened*. And at Lystra, the multitude was so enraged that they drew the apostle out of the city and *stoned* him—some say, to death (Acts 13:50; 14:5,19).

By relating these thoughts in the context of the "last days," the apostle implies that the closing days of this dispensation are going to follow the *same* course. He is merely *preparing* us for the inevitable. "Yea, and all that will live godly in Christ Jesus shall suffer persecution" (II Tim. 3:12). The persecution that the apostle speaks of here will be at the hands of ungodly men who despise the very name of Christ. So naturally the object of their wrath will

89

be directed at those who proclaim the good news of Christ and Him crucified. Undoubtedly, the first wave of oppression will be very subtle. It may simply take the form of *intolerance*. But this will quickly turn into *threats* and in some cases believers may even be called upon to be *martyrs* for Christ. Standing for the truth in the "last days" could have grave consequences. The reader must never confuse these wicked deeds of men with the wrath of God to come; they are two entirely different sets of circumstances.

Many believe that the Church will probably be driven underground before the Lord returns. Little by little, we are losing our "religious rights" even as we speak. The Bible is no longer welcome in the classroom. Prayer has been banned on school property. Many Christian schools have had to close their doors due to non-conformity to *unreasonable* regulations imposed by state and local governments. If you stand against abortion, you are an extremist and identified with those so-called radicals on the Christian right. The very tenor of these words should be cause for alarm throughout the household of God.

The time is soon coming when we may be worshipping in the catacombs of our basements, much like the 1st century believers. In the midst of this oppression which lies ahead, there is *hope!* Paul says: ". . . but out of them all [persecutions and afflictions] the Lord *delivered me*" (Vs. 11b). This promise is given to all those who are faithful in Christ Jesus. Thus, may the utterance of our lips be in accordance with the apostle: "According to my earnest expectation and my hope, that in nothing I shall be ashamed, but that with all boldness, as always, so now also Christ shall be magnified in my body, whether it be by life, or by death" (Phil. 1:20).

One Day!

One day the trumpet will sound for His coming,
  One day the skies with His glory will shine;
Wonderful day, my beloved ones bringing!
  Glorious Savior, this Jesus is mine!

Living He loved me, dying He saved me,
  Buried He carried my sins far away;
Rising He justified freely, forever:
  One day He's coming–O glorious day!

—Wilbur Chapman

5

Who is the Restrainer?

"And now ye know what withholdeth that he might
be revealed in his time. For the mystery of iniquity
doth already work: only he who now letteth will let,
until he be taken out of the way."

—*II Thessalonians 2:6,7*

Please allow me the liberty to paraphrase the above
passage to help simplify what the apostle is expressing:
"Brethren, ye already know what is restraining the Antichrist from being revealed before the tribulation. For the
spirit of lawlessness is presently at work; only he who now
hindereth the coming of the day of the Lord will hinder,
until he be taken out of the way."

To understand the tenor of Paul's words, we must first
understand the nature of the problem at Thessalonica.
We learn from the narrative that this assembly had been
infiltrated by those seeking to rob these saints of their
Blessed Hope. The poison these false teachers had poured
into their cup of deceit was a convincing message that
those at Thessalonica were in that dreaded time known as
the *day of the Lord.* In the preceding verses, Paul has
already given the antidote to this insidious teaching.
However, before leaving the matter he gave an additional
argument to ensure that this false doctrine never gained a
foothold in the assembly. The apostle informs us that

93

there is a *restraining influence* in the world that is with-holding the day of the Lord and subsequent manifestation of the Antichrist.

The large majority of dispensationalists believe that the Holy Spirit is the one hindering the man of sin's debut. If we follow this line of thought to its logical conclusion, it would be the Holy Spirit who is removed from the earth at the Rapture. However, this interpretation is inconsistent with the future ministry of the Spirit set forth in the Pro-phetic Scriptures.

THE PROMISE OF THE SPIRIT IN PROPHECY

The prophet Joel was one of the first to predict the com-ing of the Holy Spirit. This promise was later confirmed by our Lord who instructed His disciples that in His absence He would send another *Comforter.* "Even the Spirit of truth; whom the world cannot receive, because it seeth Him not, neither knoweth Him: but ye know Him; for He dwelleth *with you,* and shall be *in you*" (John 14:17). These last two phrases are very significant—not only will the Holy Spirit abide *with* them forever, He will also *indwell* the followers of Messiah, thus enabling them to endure the *future tribulation.* Peter recognized this on the day of Pentecost when he quoted Joel's prophecy con-cerning the coming of the Holy Spirit in relation to the tribulation.

> "And it shall come to pass in the last days, saith God, I will pour out of my Spirit upon all flesh: and your sons and your daughters shall prophesy, and

your young men shall see visions, and your old men shall dream dreams. . . . The sun shall be turned into darkness, and the moon into blood, before that great and notable day of the Lord come" (Acts 2:17,20).

The Spirit of God is going to play a far more dramatic role in the coming day of the Lord than He does presently in the administration of Grace. In that day, "He will reprove the world of sin, and of righteousness, and of judgment." Moreover, He will empower the tribulation saints to perform the miraculous sign gifts as a testimony of the mighty power of God (Rev. 11:3-14). Since the Spirit of truth is one of the chief participants in the coming tribulation, He could not possibly be the restrainer who is said to be removed from the earth here in II Thessalonians Chapter 2. Perhaps the visual aid on the following page will be helpful.

THE SPIRIT OF LAWLESSNESS

"Remember ye not, that, when I was yet with you, I told you these things?" (II Thes. 2:5).

"For the mystery of iniquity doth already work. . ." (II Thes. 2:7).

Shortly after the Mystery was given to Paul, Satan set into motion an evil scheme known as the "mystery of iniquity." His ultimate goal is to undermine all forms of God-ordained authority and bring the world to a state of *lawlessness.* As we approach the Lord's coming, this unrelenting attack is sure to intensify. Satan has already successfully targeted three areas that have nearly decimated our generation.

The *home* is under siege. God's original plan of authority

The Spirit's Ministry in Relation to Prophecy and the Mystery

			Disp. of Grace	Day of the Lord
Promise of the Spirit given to Israel	Promise of the Father confirmed by Christ	Coming of the Holy Spirit on the Day of Pentecost	Secret Purpose of the Holy Spirit Fulfilled Spirit Indwells Members of the Body of Christ (I Cor. 6:19,20)	Tribulation & Kingdom Fulfillment of the Promise of the Father Holy Spirit Works Signs & Wonders

Had Not the Holy Spirit's Ministry Been Interrupted By the Age of Grace It Would Have Continued Accordingly in Relation to Prophecy

Promise of the Spirit given to Israel (Joel 2:29,30)	Promise of the Father confirmed by Christ (John 14:16-20)	Coming of the Holy Spirit on the Day of Pentecost (Acts 2:1-4)	Day of the Lord
			Tribulation & Kingdom Fulfillment of the Promise of the Father Holy Spirit Works Signs & Wonders (Joel 2:30-32; Rev. 11:3-14; Ezk. 36:24-28)

that the husband is the head of the wife and children are to obey their parents has been pushed aside as old fashioned in favor of one's *rights*. The results have been catastrophic as two out of three marriages today tragically end in divorce. Children rebelliously roam the streets killing one another, as law enforcement stands helplessly by with their hands tied due to a liberal justice system. When our country lost its innocence in the 60's, God's chain of command was broken and we have been suffering the consequences ever since.

The *Church,* as well, has fallen victim to the adversary. Years ago when the town drunk passed the assembly hall where the saints were meeting, he would pause and tip his hat out of respect. Today, they leave their beer and wine bottles on our doorstep. But perhaps the most troubling trend we are witnessing is a lack of respect for the Word of God. A format of gospel music and programs is gradually replacing the sound preaching of Christ and Him crucified. Sad to say, most equate the Lord's blessing with the size of the assembly—the larger the assembly, the greater the blessing. One is hard-pressed, however, to find such a precedent in the Scriptures. Again and again, we read about the *remnant,* the *little flock* and the *church in the house.* God's blessing has always been bestowed on the basis of the *faithful* proclamation of His Word and never on mere numbers. Let the utterance of our lips forever be: "Thy Word is a lamp unto my feet, and a light unto my path" (Psa. 119:105). Moreover, believers are turning from the godly counsel of their pastors to godless psychiatrists and psychologists who do not even understand man's basic problem. Such a disregard for the authority of the Scriptures must surely grieve the heart of God.

Finally, for centuries Satan has sought to subvert the authority of *lawful government*. His most effective weapons of destruction have been corruption, dishonesty, immorality and greed. One wonders how much longer things can continue at the present rate with economic collapse, civil wars, starvation and disease threatening the existence of many nations. The world as we know it is heading for a chaotic time when confusion will reign as king.

From the ashes of despair, Satan will introduce the world to the *Great Problem Solver*. The Antichrist will have the charisma of a JFK, the intelligence and leadership abilities of a Winston Churchill, the wit of a Rush Limbaugh, the communication skills of a Ronald Reagan and the knowledge of foreign affairs of a Henry Kissinger. He will arise from obscurity to become one of history's most *infamous* leaders. Nations will be mesmerized by his uncanny ability to resolve complex problems and will, therefore, hastily align themselves with his emerging world empire. Thankfully, the *restrainer* is holding back this evil plan of Satan to take over the world.

IDENTIFYING THE RESTRAINER

If the Holy Spirit is not the restrainer, then who is this mystery person? To answer this question, we must consult the context in which our passage is set. The subject that the apostle is dealing with in II Thessalonians 2 is *our gathering together* unto the Lord (II Thes. 2:1). In verse 6, Paul makes it clear that the saints at Thessalonica knew *what* was withholding the arrival of the Antichrist. "And now ye KNOW WHAT WITHHOLDETH that he might be revealed in his time." The phrase "what withholdeth" or "that which restrains" is in the neuter gender, so at this stage of the context the apostle is not speaking of a person but an *event*. According to the narrative, the event that will trigger the circumstances of the day of the Lord is *our departure*. Thus, the Rapture of the Church must first take place before Satan can wreak havoc upon the earth.

"For the mystery of iniquity doth already work:
only he who now letteth [hindereth] will let [hinder],
until he be taken out of the way" (II Thes. 2:7).

Inasmuch as *our departure* is the overriding theme of these passages, this indicates that "he who now hindereth" could only be the *Church, the Body of Christ*. We are the restraining influence in the world that is hindering the adversary from fulfilling his wicked intentions. Personally, I do not believe that the Body of Christ is the Bride of Christ, which explains why we are never referred to in the feminine gender. This also clarifies why the apostle uses the masculine pronoun "he" in the above passage. Thus, Paul clearly identifies the pronoun *"he"* as Christ's Body of which we are members. Of course, this does not diminish from the fact that it is the Spirit's influence through the Church which enables us to be a deterrent. Nevertheless, the apostle specifies that the Body of Christ is the *restrainer*. It is with this in mind that the Church is "taken out of the way" preceding the tribulation, which cannot be said of the Holy Spirit who will play a prominent role in *things to come*.

For whatever reasons, the Church is not nearly the compelling force it once used to be. But while our voice may be weakened, we are still a voice with which to be reckoned. For example, many Christian groups around the country have been successful in closing down pornography shops in their neighborhoods. Their objections to this obscene literature has drawn attention to how detrimental this type of material can be, especially on young impressionable minds.

For the most part, it is the Christian community who has been the defender of the *right-to-life* issue by openly opposing abortion. The opposition can call it what they may, but in the sight of God abortion is **MURDER.** We may not condone all the tactics that are being used, but at least the conscience of our nation has been awakened to this senseless genocide.

Even the godless teaching of evolution, humanism and self-esteem curriculum is being challenged in our public schools. Recently a small town in Pennsylvania, led by the Christian right, demanded that the creation account be given equal time and that self-esteem classes no longer be taught. After much discussion and debate, the school board agreed.

A SOLEMN THOUGHT

A short time ago I was browsing through a Christian bookstore when a colorful pamphlet caught my eye. As I picked it up to leaf through it, I noticed that the author had portrayed the Rapture as a *chaotic* event. The pictures graphically depicted widespread pandemonium on the earth as planes fell from the sky, cars drove off cliffs and trains collided. According to this scheme of thought, tens of thousands will tragically lose their lives. But does this coincide with the Scriptures? By no means. God is not the author of confusion; He always does *everything*

100

decently and in order (I Cor. 14:33,40). For Him to do otherwise would run contrary to His nature. However, the above scenario is the epitome of MASS CONFUSION with capital letters.

Can God supernaturally stop a speeding passenger train traveling 200 m.p.h. after He raptures the operator? In the days of Joshua, God stopped the rotation of the earth on its axis one whole day so that the sun appeared to stand still for a 24 hour period (Josh. 10:12-14).[1] Which one has a greater degree of difficulty? Stopping a speeding train filled with passengers or causing the earth to cease to spin on its axis?

But what if the pilot of a 747 jetliner is taken; would not hundreds of people be killed? Not necessarily: Co-pilots are trained to land the aircraft in the event the pilot is unable to do so or in this case *unavailable*. Of course, with the advanced computer technology that we have today, jets nearly fly themselves and will probably soon have the capacity to land in like manner.

Then we have Peter, who with the help of angels, escaped from prison *twice*. Remarkably, the unsaved captors who incarcerated him were totally unaware that he was gone until hours later (Acts 5:17-28 cf. 12:1-11). Insofar as myriads of angels are at God's beck and call, they will doubtless be pressed into service when the roll is called up yonder. "Nothing is impossible with God." Therefore, we believe that God will *remove* the Body of Christ

---

1. Since those in Joshua's day were unaware that the earth orbited the sun, they perceived that it was the sun that stood still. Thus, these passages in the Book of Joshua only present the general observation of those who were there that fateful day.

from the earth without totally disrupting the balance of everyday life, as we know it.

For the sake of our loved ones, we pray that there will be one last spiritual awakening before God pours out His vengeance. Most feel that this is highly unlikely and they are probably correct, but God is "able to do exceeding abundantly above all that we ask or think." He delights in mercy and takes no pleasure in the death of the wicked. The hour is nearly upon us: "Now is the accepted time; behold, now is the day of salvation." Take Christ today; it is a decision you will never regret.

With the removal of the Body of Christ when the trump sounds, the Church's realm of influence will be withdrawn. The adversary awaits this day with great anticipation, for *lawlessness* shall be the red carpet upon which the Antichrist will make his grand entrance. Hence, Paul says, "And then shall that Wicked [one] be revealed, whom the Lord shall consume with the spirit of His mouth, and shall destroy with the brightness of His coming: Even him, whose coming is *after the working of Satan* with all power and signs and lying wonders" (II Thes. 2:8,9).

This whole chapter (II Thessalonians 2) gives further credence to the doctrine of the *pretribulational Rapture.* To say that the Body of Christ is going through any part of the seventieth week shows a failure to fully understand the distinctive character of Paul's apostleship and message. Before the Holy Spirit can resume His future prophetic ministry, we must be ushered to glory; otherwise, the two programs of God stand in jeopardy of being confused.

6

Strong Delusion

"And for this cause God shall send them strong delusion, that they should believe a lie: That they all might be damned who believed not the truth, but had pleasure in unrighteousness."

— *II Thessalonians 2:11,12*

Every year or so there seems to be someone who attempts to predict the time of the Rapture. In the late eighties, the book *88 Reasons Why the Rapture Will Occur in 1988* was a best seller. Obviously, the author was terribly mistaken. More recently, the pastor of a church in South Chicago told his congregation that the "blessed event" was to be expected on Wednesday, April 6, 1994. Many of his parishioners sold their homes and automobiles only to be left with a feeling of betrayal. Of course, the local media had a heyday ridiculing the Christian community for being gullible enough to believe such a foolish notion.

The setting of dates has been common since the recovery of the pretribulational Rapture. Those who engage themselves in this practice usually consult Old Testament prophecy to establish an elaborate numeric system of calculations based on past and present historical events. These calculations are then used to pinpoint the exact day of our Lord's return.

Other predictions are far less scientific. For example,

some teach that the generation that was alive when Israel became a state in 1948 will be the one to see the Rapture. Well, most of that generation lies in the dust of the earth and those who are yet alive have just about given up hope.

The prognosticators will *never* accurately predict the Lord's coming for the Church for this reason: *Time* in prophecy does not coincide with the present program God is carrying out, which we know to be the Mystery. When I was a little boy, we had a grandfather clock at home that occasionally stopped because someone (usually me) forgot to wind the mainspring. In similar fashion, God permitted the hands of the prophetic clock to grind to a halt with the stoning of Stephen. With prophecy at a standstill, God was free to inaugurate the dispensation of Grace which is governed by a *new standard of time.* For the past two thousand years, God has been lavishing the world with the riches of His grace, and while the hour is growing late, the time of our departure is only known to our *heavenly Father.* Insofar as the Rapture is an *unprophesied* event, it could occur tomorrow; then again, it could be fifty years from tomorrow.

The question is often raised, if the Rapture were to take place tonight would the unsaved, who will be left behind, have another opportunity to be redeemed when God's Prophetic program resumes? Some understand from Paul's words in II Thessalonians 2:8-12 that those who reject the grace of God in this dispensation will not be given a second chance in the coming day of the Lord. Perhaps a brief verse by verse exposition of the passages in question will determine whether or not this view has any merit.

104

THE LAWLESS ONE

"And then shall that Wicked be revealed, whom the Lord shall consume with the spirit of His mouth, and shall destroy with the brightness of His coming" (II Thes. 2:8).

When God starts the pendulum of the prophetic clock in motion after "our departure," the man of sin will be *immediately* revealed. *"And then shall that Wicked be revealed...."* Paul is not speaking about a state of wickedness as our translation tends to imply; rather he is unmasking the one who will deceive the world. The original here uses the *definite article;* therefore, it is the "the lawless one" that the apostle has in mind.[1] He shall be the very embodiment of evil.

Actually, we know a great deal about this one who is to come. He is said to be a beast that rises up out of the sea (Rev. 13:1). In prophecy, the sea is representative of the nations of the world. So, the Antichrist will probably rise out of a Middle East nation, such as Syria, since he is called the Assyrian (Isa. 10:3-7). Even though he comes forth from one of the Gentile nations, he will be a Hebrew by birth.[2] How else would he be able to persuade the nation Israel to believe that he is the Messiah if he were not a *son of Abraham?* But he will be a Hebrew in name only for he will not "regard the God of his fathers," which is a phrase always associated with Abraham, Isaac and Jacob (Dan. 11:35-37). Bent on self-glorification, the Antichrist will be a *bachelor* having "no regard for women." He will also be extremely wealthy and serve the god of forces (Dan. 11:37,38).

---

1. See the Textus Receptus
2. It is imperative to remember that the Jews will still be scattered abroad at the beginning of the tribulation period.

Paul substantiates this latter part when he says, "Even him, whose coming is after the working of Satan with all power and signs and lying wonders" (II Thes. 2:9). Thankfully, we shall never experience what is foretold here in II Thessalonians 2:8,9. But those believers who live through the future day of the Lord shall breathe a sigh of relief when they read about the *rise and fall* of the Antichrist in the same context. In these passages under consideration, there are *two comings* and *two sons*.

First is the *coming* of the *son of perdition* (Antichrist) at the beginning of the tribulation. Inasmuch as the natural man is so easily given over to emotional experience, the "son of perdition" will use this to his advantage. On his rise to world acclaim, he will deceive men by means of ". . . power and signs and lying wonders" (Vs. 9).

Israel had a rich history when it came to *signs* and *wonders*. They were often used by God to *confirm* the testimony of His Word. Thus, when the scribes and Pharisees "would *see* a sign" the Lord refused to satisfy their flare for the dramatic. He did, however, give them the *sign of the prophet Jonah* as *confirmation* of His death, burial and resurrection. Just as Jonah was three days in the belly of the great fish, so the Son of Man was three days and three nights in the heart of the earth (Matt. 12:38-40). Furthermore, as Jonah plunged to the depths of the sea, he was *alive* and prayed for deliverance, which foreshadowed the Lord's activity during His entombment (Jonah 2:1-7 cf. I Peter 3:18-20).

The man of sin will be well aware that the "Jews require a sign" and gladly accommodate their curiosity. In that day,

106

men will not believe their eyes when they see fire come down from heaven and the Antichrist rise from the dead after suffering a mortal wound. With their senses dulled to that which is right, they will follow this Deceiver to the ends of the earth in rebellion against the true and living God.

In the coming day of the Lord, Satan goes out of his way to *counterfeit* the things of God. This is clearly seen in his desire to establish the Satanic trinity—the *dragon* (Satan) represents God the Father; the *beast* (Antichrist) represents God the Son; and the *false prophet* (second beast) represents God the Holy Spirit (Rev. 13:4-12 cf. 20:10). Needless to say, the miracles performed by the Antichrist and his subsequent return from the dead are mere counterfeits of our Lord's miracles and resurrection from the dead. Blinded by these miraculous manifestations, the world will wonder after the beast and actually believe that he is the Messiah who is sent from God.

The other *coming* addressed by the apostle is that of the *Son of Man* who returns at the close of the tribulation to destroy the Antichrist (II Thes. 2:8). The day has already been appointed when the false Messiah will come face to face with the *true* Messiah on the plain of Megiddo. Christ will slay the Antichrist with the *breath* of His mouth and end his reign of terror. He is then sentenced to a life of torment in the lake of fire. Amazingly, one thousand years *after* his encounter with Christ at Armageddon, John saw Satan ". . . cast into the lake of fire and brimstone, WHERE THE BEAST and the false prophet ARE, and shall be tormented day and night forever and ever" (Rev. 20:10).

THE ANTICHRIST'S SEAT OF AUTHORITY

Before we leave this topic, perhaps we should pinpoint the precise area of the world that the Antichrist will establish his *seat of authority*. Since *Babylon* is undoubtedly the city from which the man of sin will reign, the following two questions are frequently raised concerning its restoration to her ancient glory. How do we explain the future rebuilding of Babylon in view of Isaiah 13, which teaches that after its destruction, it was never to be inhabited nor dwelt in from generation to generation? Isn't the Babylon spoken of in the Book of Revelation to be understood symbolically as being political and ecclesiastical Rome?

a. The Twofold Purpose of Prophecy

"And Babylon, the glory of kingdoms, the beauty of the Chaldees' excellency, shall be as when God overthrew Sodom and Gomorrah" (Isa. 13:19).

"And they shall not take of thee [Babylon] a stone for a corner, nor a stone for foundations; but thou shalt be desolate for ever, saith the Lord" (Jer. 51:26).

The fulfillment of many Old Testament prophecies often has a short and long term significance. For example, in Isaiah 61:2, we find these words: *To proclaim the acceptable year of the Lord, and the day of vengeance of our God.* . . ." Upon entering the synagogue at Nazareth, our Lord was handed the Book of Isaiah from which He read the portion, "To proclaim the acceptable year of the Lord." He then closed the Book and said, "This day is this Scripture fulfilled in your ears" (Luke 4:21). Inasmuch as the remainder of this passage was not to be fulfilled until a later time, our Lord avoided associating His hearers

108

with the "day of vengeance," and appropriately so! The passage demonstrates that many prophesies have a *twofold* purpose.

We believe the destruction of *Babylon* falls into this category as well. There is little question that Isaiah and Jeremiah foretold the impending doom of this treasured city of gold. But has every detail of these prophesies literally been fulfilled? Surely not! Historically, we know that ancient Babylon existed many years after the fall of the empire. Yet Jeremiah spoke of her fall as being *sudden.* Although this prophecy was unfulfilled in time past, the Apostle John reveals in the Book of Revelation that *future* Babylon will be destroyed in *one day* (Jer. 51:8 cf. Rev. 18:8).

In addition, Isaiah compares her ruin to the cities of *Sodom* and *Gomorrah.* While calamity did, indeed, befall the Babylon of old, the one yet to come shall be destroyed by fire and brimstone much like the cities of the plain. In similar fashion, it quite literally will be wiped off the face of the earth and be found no more (Isa. 13:19; Jer. 51:26; Rev. 18:8,9,18,21). Those who methodically search the Scriptures will agree that this calls for a *futuristic* interpretation. The evidence surely leads us to conclude that this rendering is correct insofar as there was a *church* located at Babylon in Peter's day (I Peter 5:13). Furthermore, unlike Sodom and Gomorrah, tourists still take pilgrimages to visit the image of Nebuchadnezzar and to observe the results of other archeological findings. Perhaps the most convincing argument that Babylon will be restored is cradled in the words of the prophet. Isaiah pinpoints the fulfillment of this prophecy as taking place in the *day of the Lord* when the heavens are darkened

(Isa. 13:1,6-11). This, of course, corroborates that the "golden city" must rise again from the ashes of history only to experience a more devastating fall the second time.

b. The Location of the Seat of Authority

We believe it is imperative to distinguish between the city of Babylon and its political and ecclesiastical counterparts. The traditional view of the Church has been that the Antichrist's seat of authority will be Rome. Scriptures to support such a position, however, are nonexistent.

The Prophet Daniel vividly describes for us the past Gentile world empires, each of which were basically centered in the *Middle East*. History bears out the amazing accuracy of his prophecy as the lion represents *Babylon;* the bear, *Media Persia* followed by the leopard whom we now know to be *Alexander the Great's* kingdom (Dan. 7:3-6). The last beast that Daniel saw in his vision was "dreadful and terrible, and strong exceedingly" (Dan. 7:7). This is clearly a reference to the future *Antichrist kingdom*. The former Gentile world empires all succeeded each other and each expanded their boundaries far beyond their predecessors. Therefore, we are to understand that the Antichrist's kingdom will follow suit. It will embody the greatness of the ancient empires and be located in the same vicinity—the Middle East!

We are well aware that many Bible teachers believe this *fourth world empire* to be Rome and that the Antichrist's kingdom will merely be the revival of the old Roman Empire. Since this view holds such wide acceptance in the Christian community, the reader is wise to weigh this position carefully. However, this interpretation has an *insurmountable problem*: The Word of God explicity states that the fourth kingdom will be destroyed by the *Second Coming of Christ* (Dan. 2:44,45; 7:9-14 cf. Rev. 19:11-19). This cannot be said of the Roman empire by any stretch of the imagination. Rome decayed gradually from within over a period of many years.

In Revelation 13:1,2 the beast and his kingdom which rise up out of the sea are said to be ". . . like unto a *leopard,* and his feet were as the feet of a *bear,* and his mouth as the mouth of a *lion....*" Obviously, these individual kingdoms of ancient times are going to be *revived* in the future tribulation. But in that day there will be an *amalgamation* of these former kingdoms into a *world empire,* the likes of which has never been seen before. Subsequently, the Antichrist will reign from the city of *Babylon* which is strategically situated in the *Middle East. Babylon,* then, will be his seat of authority from which will flow a one-world government and a one-world religion (Rev. 13:7,8).

Satan's new world order will cover the territory of Alexander's kingdom, have the political power of Media Persia, and rule with the iron-fisted authority of an ancient Babylon. So then, God's Word points us to the *east,* not to Rome and the European nations, although they will most certainly play a secondary role.

THE PASSING OF GRACE

"And with all deceivableness of unrighteousness in them that perish; because they receive not the love of the truth, that they might be saved" (II Thes. 2:10).

As we pass from the dispensation of Grace to the *dis-*

111

pensation of Divine Government the change is going to be *abrupt.* There will not be a transition period at the close of this dispensation as there was at the beginning of it. When the last member is placed into the Body of Christ and the fullness of the Gentiles has come in, the gospel of the grace of God will be proclaimed no longer. Following our homegoing, God will reinstate the *kingdom gospel* at the dawn of the tribulation.

> "And this gospel of the kingdom shall be preached in all the world for a witness unto all nations; and then shall the end come" (Matt. 24:14).

In this context then, the *truth* that men refuse to receive that they might be saved is not the gospel of grace, rather it is the *kingdom gospel.* It is our firm conviction that those who are left behind after our departure will be given another chance to be *saved* in the age to come. This is in keeping with the very nature of God who is rich in *mercy* and ". . . not willing that any should perish, but that all should come to repentance" (II Peter 3:9). In all probability, the majority of those who fail to receive Christ under grace will continue in their unbelief. Nevertheless, the *door of salvation* will remain open, although it will be much more difficult for a Gentile to be saved since the terms of the kingdom gospel are far more *involved.*

According to what the Apostle Paul says here in II Thessalonians, the Antichrist through the "deceivableness of unrighteousness" will bring men to the precipice of eternal damnation. He will use every form of deception imaginable to turn men away from the truth that Jesus Christ is *God* and therefore the rightful *heir* to the throne of David. But not only will the man of sin lead men away

112

from the "love of the truth," the phraseology here seems to suggest that they will have an *aversion* to it. Consequently, this is what awaits those who *believe* during the day of the Lord: "Then shall they deliver you up to be afflicted, and shall kill you: and ye shall be hated of all nations for my name's sake" (Matt. 24:9).

WILL THERE BE A LULL BEFORE THE STORM?

There has been quite a spirited discussion of late as to whether or not there will be a brief *interlude* preceding the day of the Lord. Those who defend this theory believe that there could be a period as long as one year before the actual events of the tribulation occur. While this may be an interesting concept to ponder, it lacks any type of Scriptural support. One thing I have learned: "If any man speak, let him speak as the oracles of God..." (I Peter 4:11).

We believe that the Rapture will be followed *immediately* by the time of Jacob's trouble. Inasmuch as the Scriptures do not indicate that there will be a "lull before the storm," we can safely conclude that God's Prophetic program will resume where it left off in Acts 7:54-60. The stoning of Stephen would have marked the beginning of the tribulation had it not been for the *secret purpose* of God known as the Mystery. Prior to this interruption, the Son of Man was depicted as *standing* at the right hand of the Father preparing to execute judgment upon His enemies (Psa. 7:6). Interestingly, when prophecy resumes, the first thing John beholds when he is transported to the future day of the Lord is the Son of Man *standing* in the midst of the seven kingdom churches in Asia (Rev. 1:12-18).

God has never left Himself without a testimony on the earth to bring His plan of salvation to those who so desperately need it. When He moved from the kingdom gospel to the gospel of grace there was *no* interval between these two gospels which would have placed men in danger of eternal damnation. This will also be true when the dispensation of Grace closes. If there is a year sabbatical following the Rapture as some suppose, then God would be left *without* a witness on the earth. Furthermore, if a sinner were to die during this period, he would be justified in leveling the charge that he could not have been saved even if he had wanted to be.

Since every believer will be removed from the earth at the Rapture, it will be necessary for God to *immediately* graft Israel back into the olive tree. She will again proclaim the kingdom gospel, thus fulfilling every detail of the Great Commission (Matt. 24:14; Acts 1:8 cf. Rom. 11:16-24).

But how do we address the problem this creates with Daniel 9:27 where it is clear that the *temple* must be in existence at the *beginning* of the tribulation? We acknowledge that the sacrificial system will be immediately reinstated following our departure. There is a remote possibility that Israel could try to restore the Levitical system in her own strength decades before the Rapture takes place. It is a well-known fact that she has already secured the materials that would be needed to rebuild the temple. Of course, any attempt to accomplish this today would be *futile* in the sight of God. However, when the Prophetic program resumes, the glory of the Lord could fill the edifice wherein God would again honor the offerings of His people.

114

It seems far more likely that upon our homegoing Israel (under God's direction) will erect a temporary *tabernacle* (tent) similar to the one that was used during the years she wandered in the wilderness (Ex. 26,27). This would facilitate the reinstatement of the sacrificial system in the shadow of the temple mound. Inasmuch as this structure (temple) could be built in a matter of months, it seems reasonable that the furniture in the tabernacle could merely be transferred to the temple, as in the days of Solomon (I Kings 8:3-11).

THE DAY AFTER

As the sound of the trump fades in the heavens, the last seven years of Daniel's seventy weeks of years will make their debut. In conjunction with the rebuilding of the temple, God will launch the tribulation by sending His *two witnesses* to the earth to *evangelize* the one hundred forty-four thousand from all of the twelve tribes of Israel (Rev. 7:4-8). Although there has been some speculation as to the identity of these two witnesses, we believe that *Moses* and *Elijah* are probably in view because they are frequently mentioned together in relation to *things to come* (Mal. 4:1-6; Matt. 16:28; 17:1-5 cf. Rev. 11:3-8).

Most commentators insist that the ministry of Moses and Elijah covers the last three and one-half years of the tribulation. However, a close examination of the record clearly places their ministry during the first half of this period. There are *three woes* outlined for us in the Apocalypse (Rev. 8:13). When the Antichrist ascends out of the bottomless pit he slays the two witnesses, which brings to pass the *second woe*. This particular judgment is in the form of an earthquake which destroys a tenth part

115

of the city of Jerusalem and kills seven thousand men (Rev. 11:13,14). Insofar as the *third woe* is yet to follow near the end of the tribulation, we are to understand that the two witnesses will live and serve the Lord at the *beginning* of the day of the Lord. Furthermore, Chapters 11,12,13 and 14 of the Book of Revelation describe the *mid-part* of Daniel's seventieth week, not the latter part.

In summary, the day of the Lord begins as a time of *peace* and *safety* as the Antichrist puts into place his master plan to rule the world (I Thes. 5:1-3). In the meantime, the two witnesses evangelize the 144,000 from the twelve tribes. They, in turn, fulfill the Great Commission, evangelizing Jerusalem, Judaea, Samaria and the world of the Gentiles. Thousands will come to Messiah in that day as the kingdom gospel reaches every corner of the earth (Matt. 24:14 cf. Rev. 7:9-17). During this brief time of peace, the Son of Man will minister to the seven churches in Asia who are representative of the *kingdom church* in general. The Judge of all the earth commends these assemblies on one hand and on the other chastens them for their unbelief. But the most solemn thought of all is His warning that they are living in the day of His *wrath* (Rev. 1:9 cf. 6:17).

Will there be a *lull before the storm rages? NO!* We believe God will shift from the dispensation of Grace back to His Prophetic program without missing a heartbeat.

THE LIE

"And for this cause God shall send them strong delusion, that they should believe a lie" (II Thes. 2:11).

As we have seen, during the first three and one-half years of the future holocaust, God will temper His judgment with mercy, giving men an opportunity to be converted. However, when their hearts wax cold with hatred against the truth near the middle of the tribulation, "God shall send them *strong delusion* that they should believe a lie." Strong delusion, that is, in the sense of a *working of error.* God will not send them error per se, but He will permit them to merely slip farther and farther into the wickedness they have deliberately chosen. Much like the Gentiles of old when they turned the truth of God into a lie: "God gave them *up* unto vile affections. . . . And even as they did not like to retain God in their knowledge, God gave them *over* to a reprobate mind, to do those things which are not convenient [fitting]" (Rom. 1:26-28).

Hopelessly lost men will foolishly believe *the lie* in that day and recklessly plunge themselves into eternal damnation.[3] What is this *lie* that places men in such jeopardy? It is the crown jewel of all "deceivableness of unrighteousness" masterfully crafted by the Antichrist. In the middle of Daniel's seventieth week, the man of sin will enter into the temple at Jerusalem and brazenly declare himself to be God. This is the *abomination of desolation* (Matt. 24:15 cf. II Thes. 2:4). Those who believe this *lie* and receive the mark of the beast will be eternally doomed without hope of reprieve.

The *mark of the beast* will give the Antichrist total control over the populace, ensuring their allegiance to his cause. It probably will be some type of *micro chip* or

---

3. Once again, something definite is in view i.e. "that which is *false*" or "*the lie*". See the Textus Receptus.

indelible mark on the forehead and right hand that can easily be scanned. Without it no one will be able to buy or sell, which implies that God will have to supernaturally supply for His own to enable them to survive the latter part of Jacob's trouble. Those who refuse to receive this mark will doubtless be executed on the spot. Thus, few, if any, are saved in the great tribulation!

The foregoing helps us to better understand Paul's closing words: "That they all might be damned who believed not the truth [kingdom gospel], but had pleasure in unrighteousness." Little wonder the apostle begged men everywhere to trust Christ as their Savior. He knew that in the future day of the Lord men would be preoccupied with merely trying to survive, giving little or no thought to their lost condition.

Perhaps there is a loved one that you have been meaning to talk to about the Lord but haven't gotten around to as yet. Please, do it today, you may just spare them from being exposed to the reign of deception and terror that lies ahead.

7

Our Blessed Hope

"Looking for that blessed hope, and the glorious appearing of the great God and our Savior Jesus Christ."

—*Titus 2:13*

There is nothing more terrible than to be without *hope!* Historically, the Gentiles found themselves in this very state preceding the age of Grace: ". . . because that, when they knew God, they glorified Him not as God." For nearly two thousand years, they wandered aimlessly through a *hopeless* existence, while Israel enjoyed the glory of God's presence. We were ". . . strangers from the covenants of promise, having no hope, and without God in the world: But now in Christ Jesus ye who sometimes were far off are made nigh by the blood of Christ" (Eph. 2:12,13).

Thankfully, on the dark and stormy seas of life the Gentiles can again see the *hope of salvation* from the lighthouse of divine grace. Tragically though, many are unwilling to follow the Light to safe harbor, preferring rather to remain lost at sea! What profit is God's gracious offer of salvation if one refuses to believe it? He is no better off than his forebearers who were denied access to the gospel. This hopeless condition is a mere reflection of an inscription discovered on a grave site at Thessalonica: "After death there is no revival, after the grave no meeting of those who have loved each other on earth." In Paul's day this philosophy was common throughout the Roman Empire, which undoubtedly had some bearing on a question that arose at Thessalonica concerning "life after death."

THE AWAKENING

"But I would not have you to be ignorant, brethren, concerning them which are asleep, that ye sorrow not, even as others which have no hope" (I Thes. 4:13).

As newborn babes grow in the faith, there are hundreds of questions that naturally race across their minds. Of course, every answer they receive, based upon the Scriptures, is a stepping stone to a higher plateau of spiritual growth. Those at Thessalonica experienced this very thing shortly after their conversion to Christ. It was Paul's custom to evangelize the unsaved and then commit unto them the truth of the pretribulational Rapture. This same pattern was followed at Thessalonica, but insofar as time was of the essence, Paul had to depart from the city before these saints were completely grounded in this wonderful truth.

The cost of being a Christian back in those days was extremely high; consequently, we can only conclude that some suffered martyrdom for the cause of Christ not long after Paul moved on to Athens (I Cor. 7:26-31). Others may have had loved ones who were near death upon the apostle's arrival and gladly believed and rejoiced in the "Blessed Hope." Whatever the case may be, it is clear that some of their number had passed through the valley of death, which raised a number of legitimate concerns. "Will we ever see our loved ones again?" "Has God made a

120

special provision for them?" "What part, if any, will they have in the Rapture?"

There is no clear indication that those at Thessalonica had written Paul on the fate of their loved ones. But we do know that after their conversion the apostle had sent Timothy from Athens to further establish them in the faith (I Thes. 3:1,2). So, it was probably young Timothy who had brought word to the apostle informing him of these new circumstances. This prompted Paul to write his first epistle, leaving us the most cherished portion of Holy Scripture ever written on the subject of our *Blessed Hope*.

He begins this beloved portion by saying: *"But I would not have you to be ignorant, brethren, concerning them which are asleep...."* The apostle used this phraseology no less than six times in his epistles, each of which marks a particular turning point in the context it is found. Paul does not mean to imply by using this expression that his readers were simpletons. Rather, he is pointing out the fact that they simply lacked knowledge on the *intermediate state* of the dead.

In relation to the members of the Body of Christ, the intermediate state is that time between *death* and the *secret resurrection* when the Lord descends from heaven with a shout. When this earthly tabernacle is overpowered by the icy grip of death, the soul and spirit immediately exit the body. Death is merely the *separation* of the immaterial part of our being from this earthly house. Thus, to be absent from the body is to be present with the Lord (II Cor. 5:6-8). However, this is an *incomplete* state, for they, too, await the sound of the trump to receive their

121

glorified resurrected bodies. So then, those who have gone on before us are alive and well in a disembodied state.

These are the ones who are said to be "asleep in Jesus." This is clearly a reference to the *physical body* which lies in the dust of the earth. While there are those who hold the theological position that the soul sleeps in death, this is surely not the teaching of the Word of God. For example:

> "And it came to pass after these things, that the son [widow's son of Zarephath] of the woman, the mistress of the house, fell sick; and his sickness was so sore, that there was no breath left in him [i.e. he died]. And he [Elijah] stretched himself upon the child three times, and cried unto the Lord, and said, O Lord my God, I pray Thee, let this child's soul come into him again. And the Lord heard the voice of Elijah; and the SOUL OF THE CHILD CAME INTO HIM AGAIN, and he revived" (I Kings 17:17,21,22).

> "And when He [Christ] had opened the fifth seal, I [John] SAW under the altar the souls of them that were slain for the Word of God, and for the testimony which they held: And they cried with a LOUD VOICE, saying, How long, O Lord, holy and true, dost Thou not judge and avenge our blood on them that dwell on the earth?" (Rev. 6:9,10).

It is the *body* that has the appearance of being asleep in death, not the soul, as some have erroneously taught. Some golden daybreak, the bodies of the saints shall be *awakened* out of their sleep and rise forevermore! Hence, the apostle could console those at Thessalonica that even though they had laid their loved ones to rest, they were to ". . . *sorrow not, even as others which have no hope.*" Believers have the assurance that their departed loved

122

ones are *presently* with the Lord. Believers have the hope of a future *resurrection.* Believers have the hope of *reunion;* that is, they shall see *again* their mothers, fathers, brothers and sisters who are in Christ. Believers have the hope of *heaven.* Believers have the hope of *eternal life.*

But there are some among us who have failed to familiarize themselves with these blessed truths, which has had devastating consequences. There is a *proper* and an *improper* way to respond when death unexpectedly claims one who is close to us. It is quite natural for us to grieve the passing of a loved one. Often the tears will flow like a river as a sense of loss seems to permeate every fiber of our being. Even the Scriptures instruct us to "weep with them that weep." Paul cautions us, however, not to sorrow as others who have no hope. In other words, we are not to sorrow to the point of despair.

When an unbeliever loses a family member, death, in their mind, is the final curtain. There is no life beyond the grave. Thus, their philosophy of life can be summed up in these words: "Eat, drink and be merry, for tomorrow we die." They casually speak of heaven and hell, but if they really believed there were such places, they would receive God's gracious offer of salvation without delay. Little wonder when the grim reaper visits them they become so despondent. Their "wailing of despair" can sometimes be heard throughout the funeral home and it is nearly impossible to console them. Tranquilizers may dull the emotions, *but they will never be a remedy for a hopeless condition.*

Death will also visit the household of God, but our

response should be much different from that of the unsaved. I have stood by the casket with many believers in my lifetime and I know their hearts were breaking; nevertheless, they laid claim to the above promises. Through it all, they were a wonderful testimony and glorified God in the process. When the grim reaper robs you of a godly mother, your initial response should be: I am so thankful my mother is with the Lord. And although she will be deeply missed, I know I shall *see her again.*

You may be thinking: But Pastor, I fear that when that time arrives I will fall to pieces and disgrace my Lord. If you are *prepared* beforehand, God often extends a special measure of grace to those who call upon Him. You may have doubts now, but in that day God ". . . is able to do exceeding abundantly above all that we ask or think, according to the power that worketh in us." The evening before John Huss was to be burned at the stake, he placed his hand over the open flame of a candle only to withdraw it with haste. He wept openly, convinced he would dishonor the Lord. The following day when he was executed, it is said, he left this life singing hymns and glorifying God. Indeed, God's grace is sufficient in time of need; however, *He determines when that time is!*

A DIVINE PATTERN

"For if we believe that Jesus died and rose again, even so them also which sleep in Jesus will God bring with Him. For this we say unto you by the Word of the Lord, that we which are alive and remain unto the coming of the Lord shall not prevent [precede] them which are asleep" (I Thes. 4:14,15).

124

Paul stated in his early ministry that he would ". . . come to visions and revelations in the Lord." Because the teaching of the Rapture was *purposely excluded* from the Prophetic Scriptures, a special revelation was necessary to impart the various details of this coming. One of the first things to strike our attention is that the terms of salvation have *changed* for this dispensation.

Since the dawn of civilization, landmarks have been used to determine the boundaries of a tract of land. In similar fashion, with the introduction of the Mystery, God set new boundaries which clearly identify where the age of Grace *begins* and *ends.* We might look at it like this: Prior to Paul's revelation, the kingdom gospel required that a sinner "repent and be baptized" for the remission of his sins. With the raising up of the Apostle Paul, those who live in this age must believe Christ *died* for their sins, was *buried,* and *rose again.* We are forgiven by His shed blood. After our departure, the terms of salvation will revert back to the kingdom gospel.

This means that only those who are redeemed under Paul's gospel are members of the Body of Christ and, therefore, partakers of the heavenly hope. We conclude, then, that the two landmarks of grace are *Paul's conversion* and the *Rapture of the Church.* In the Old Testament, there were severe consequences imposed upon those who moved a landmark. Surely, the same will be true of those who tamper with the boundaries set down by God to merely accommodate a midtribulation position.

It must have been very consoling to those at Thessalonica to learn that when their loved ones had believed Paul's gospel it gave them a position in Christ that could never be altered. Interestingly, the apostle seems to establish a *divine pattern* for us. Christ died and rose again, *in that order.* Paul's fundamental declaration that "they were to sorrow not" is based on an understanding that, like Christ, their loved ones have died, but they shall also be *raised* from the dead in like manner.

"Even so them also which sleep in Jesus will God bring with Him." This passage gives us further confirmation that the "dead in Christ" are in the *presence* of the Lord. How else could God bring them with Him if they are not in heaven in the first place! We believe that those who have died in Christ over the past two thousand years are *serving* the Lord and looking forward to the fulfillment of the "Blessed Hope" as much as we are. Perhaps heaven is astir even as you read these words, for soon the Lord will lead them out of heaven where they shall appear with Him in glory (Col. 3:4).

Of course, this is our hope as well, but God does everything decently and in order as we shall go on to see.

THREE VOICES FROM HEAVEN

"For the Lord Himself shall descend from heaven with a shout, with the voice of the archangel, and with the trump of God: and the dead in Christ shall rise first" (I Thes. 4:16).

Most of us have been richly blessed with the gift of hearing. Thus, during the course of any given day, we are bombarded with a wide range of sounds, each of which serves a purpose. For example, there are sounds that warn us of approaching danger. If we hear the shrill whistle of an oncoming train, we stop, look and *listen* to avoid

126

bodily injury. In the event our smoke detector is set off in the middle of the night, the alarm warns us to flee from harm's way. These are only two of the hundreds of ways our hearing keeps us from falling victim to a tragedy.

Although the sounds we hear in life are as diverse as snowflakes, there are three particular sounds that every believer anxiously awaits at the Rapture. They are *three voices* that shall be heard from heaven when this glorious event takes place. Each *utterance* is identified with a unique phase of the Rapture, which ultimately will bring the whole Body of Christ together for the first time since its creation.

Our readers will recall when the Syrians surrounded the camp of Israel in the days of Elisha that defeat appeared to be imminent. When Elisha's servant rose up early in the morning and saw the great host that was preparing to descend upon them, he said to his master: "How shall we do?" In other words, "What in the world are we going to do now?" With sure death staring this young man in the face, Elisha calmly replied:

> "Fear not: for they that be with us are more than they that be with them. And Elisha prayed, and said, Lord, I pray Thee, open his eyes, that he may see. And the Lord opened the eyes of the young man; and he saw: and, behold, the mountain was full of horses and chariots of fire round about Elisha" (II Kings 6:16,17).

It is my personal conviction that the Body of Christ is going to have a similar experience. Our eyes will also be opened to the spiritual realm, enabling us to *see* and *hear* every aspect of the Rapture. We look forward to this blessed event with great anticipation, insofar as the sorrows of this life will be left behind. Then we shall rejoice in the *Triumph of His Grace* forevermore. But, what could possibly be the significance of these three heavenly *voices?*

a. The Shout

"For the Lord Himself shall descend from heaven with a shout" (I Thes. 4:16).

The first *voice* we will hear when the time of our departure arrives is that of our Lord. There seems to be good reason to believe that this *shout* from the heavenly realm is to summon the *dead in Christ* from their graves. This conclusion is based on the circumstances surrounding the first resurrection taught in prophecy. Preceding the millennium, the Son of Man is said to *call* forth believing Israel from the dust of the earth. "Marvel not at this: for the hour is coming, in the which all that are in the graves shall HEAR His voice, and shall come forth; they that have done good, unto the resurrection of life. . ." (John 5:28,29a).

There is power in that voice, power to raise the dead! This is demonstrated for us in the raising of Lazarus from the dead, which foreshadows the first resurrection. As we know, our Lord had deliberately delayed His coming to heal His friend so that the Father might be glorified. By the time He arrived in Bethany, Lazarus had already died. Mary and Martha believed in the future resurrection of Israel, but nothing could have prepared them for what was about to occur. After the stone was rolled away from their brother's tomb, the Giver of Life "cried with a LOUD VOICE, Lazarus, come forth" (John 11:43). It was a good thing that the Lord identified His friend by name; otherwise, as some have suggested, all of the dead may have come walking out of their resting places.

128

Of course, we must be very careful never to confuse our resurrection with the first resurrection; they are two entirely separate events. But since God does everything decently and in order, the above does seem to suggest that perhaps the resurrections will follow the same *pattern* in the two programs of God. Thus, when the dead in Christ hear the *shout* here in I Thessalonians 4:16, they will instantaneously receive their glorified resurrected bodies. Then the Scripture will be fulfilled that the "dead in Christ shall rise first: then we which are alive and remain shall be caught up together with them in the clouds. . . ." Unlike believing Israel who marches into Zion when she is raised, the members of Christ's Body shall be transported via the Rapture into the heavens. Hence, the dead in Christ who are presently in a disembodied state, eagerly wait for that *shout* from glory to—**COME FORTH!**

b. A Call To Arms

". . . with the voice of the archangel. . ." (I Thes. 4:16).

As the drama of our redemption unfolds, like most dramas, there is a supporting cast. In the beginning when Lucifer fell, by reason of his wisdom and beauty, he and the fallen host of angels who rebelled with him were banished from the presence of a holy God. Consequently, they were confined to the first and second heavens. Paul says: "For we wrestle not against flesh and blood, but against principalities, against powers, against the rulers of the darkness of this world, against spiritual wickedness in high [or heavenly] places" (Eph. 6:12). This means that the *road to glory* passes through enemy territory.

Let's suppose for a moment that you are the commander of a large military unit in the South Seas. Unexpectedly, you receive a call from the "Top Brass" instructing you that a small platoon on the other side of the island needs reinforcements immediately. Time does not permit you to go around the island, therefore, your troops must cut directly across it, even though it is heavily infiltrated with enemy forces. Now, do you think that they are going to sit idly by and watch your unit march to the other side of the island? Why, there are going to be more gun barrels pointed at you than you could shake a stick at! Obviously, the enemy will stop at nothing to hinder your crossing.

It is hard to imagine that Satan and his rulers of darkness would permit us to pass through their domain without a battle royal. Thus, to ensure our safety, the *voice* of the archangel will *call to arms* the elect angels of God. Of course, in the future time of Jacob's trouble the archangel will be the one who stands in defense of the children of Israel (Dan. 12:1). In fact, during the middle of the tribulation, Michael and his angels will wage an *offensive* campaign to cast out the Devil and his angels from the heavenly realm that rightfully belongs to us. For the present, however, the angels of God are carrying on a ministry to the Body of Christ which is highlighted by the presence of the archangel at our homegoing. The elect angels are ministers to all those who are heirs of salvation, including the members of the Body of Christ (Rom. 8:17-25; Eph. 3:10 cf. Heb. 1:13,14).

So then, on the day of our departure from planet Earth, the *voice* of the archangel will rally the angelic host in a *defensive* campaign guaranteeing our safe passage

130

through enemy territory (Eph. 6:12 cf. Rev. 12:7-12). Thankfully, we are going to be changed in a moment, in the twinkling of an eye; otherwise, we would probably be paralyzed with fear. If you can picture the amazement of Elisha's servant when his eyes were opened to the spiritual realm, you have some idea as to the startling sights and sounds we are sure to see and hear at the Rapture.

c. The Voice of God

". . . with the trump of God. . . (I Thes. 4:16).

When Moses approached the Lord to receive the Law at Mount Sinai the record states, "when the *voice of the trumpet* sounded long, and waxed louder and louder, Moses spake, and God answered him by a voice" (Ex. 19:19). The Apostle John relates a similar experience in the Apocalypse: "I was in the Spirit on the Lord's day, and heard behind me a great *voice, as of a trumpet*" (Rev. 1:10). Whether or not we are to understand this as being the actual voice of God or merely the sound of a trumpet is difficult to ascertain. Consequently, we shall leave the final outcome with the reader. Whatever the case may be, we do know the *sound* that permeates the heavens when the Lord returns will be that of a *trumpet*.

"In a moment, in the twinkling of an eye, at the last trump: for the trumpet shall sound, and the dead shall be raised incorruptible, and we shall be changed" (I Cor. 15:52).

"And the seventh angel sounded; and there were great voices in heaven, saying, the kingdoms of this world are become the kingdoms of our Lord. . ." (Rev. 11:15).

The above passages are often used by the midtribul-

131

tionists to prove that the Church the Body of Christ will go through at least part of the tribulation period. To support this theory, they claim that the "last trump" of Paul's epistle is synonymous with the blowing of the "seventh trumpet" in the day of the Lord. In essence, they are saying, "We know that the 'last trump' is closely identified with the Church, therefore, since it is not blown until Revelation 11:15, it logically follows that the Church will go midway through the time of Jacob's trouble." They further inquire, "How can you possibly contend that the last trump will sound prior to the seventh trumpet? If any other trumpets sound after it, how can it be called the last trump?" To a great extent, their position stands or falls on this basic premise.

Once again, this entire issue is resolved by simply distinguishing between *Prophecy* and the *Mystery*. The *last trump* closes God's Mystery program resulting in the removal of the Church in *blessing,* whereas the *seventh trumpet* of the Apocalypse is sounded in *judgment.* Where Paul's writings leave off, the Prophetic writings continue, taking the reader into the future day of the Lord. Subsequently, the primary purpose of the Book of Revelation is to give us a chronology of the judgments to come. Three major judgments loom on the horizon which are identified as the *seal, trumpet* and *bowl judgments,* each of which runs in a sequence of seven.

Perhaps we should pause here to illustrate the difference between "last in a point of time" and "last in a sequence." A school day is normally brought to a close by the *last bell* of the day (last in a point of time). The next day follows with seven bells being sounded in a sequence

132

at the beginning of each class. The seventh bell in this context would be the "last in the sequence" to be followed by the final bell of the day. In like fashion, the Apostle Paul uses the phrase "last trump" in the sense of *last in a point of time* when he refers to the close of this dispensation. On the other hand, the seven trumpets of the Apocalypse are unveiled in the context of a *sequence,* the last of this series of seven being followed by the bowl judgments. It should be further noted that *all* seven trumpets are sounded by *seven angels* whereas the trumpet that will be heard at the Rapture is identified as the *trump of God* (Rev. 8; 9; 11:15 cf. I Thes. 4:16).

The blowing of the seventh trumpet yields the seven bowl judgments, the last of which (seventh bowl) coincides with the Second Coming of Christ at the *end* of the Great Tribulation.

> "And He shall send His angels with a great sound of a trumpet, and they shall gather together His elect from the four winds, from one end of heaven to the other" (Matt. 24:31).

According to God's prophetic calendar, the angels will sound the trumpets *once again* preceding the millennial kingdom. This, of course, will be in fulfillment of the Levitical *Feast of Trumpets* which typified the day when Israel would be *regathered* into the Promised Land. Israel's hope is that she will one day walk with her Messiah in the land that was promised to Abraham.

Bringing our thoughts back to the *Trump of God,* Paul makes it quite clear that this phrase is exclusively identified with the Rapture of the Church. Thus, when the *trump* sounds, it will be God's unforgettable way of *gather-*

133

ing both the dead in Christ and we who are alive and remain into His presence. The Body of Christ is divided today in many ways, but in that day we shall all be *one* in the truest meaning of the word. Amen!

8

Is the Rapture Taught in the Four Gospels?

"Now I say that Jesus Christ was a minister of the circumcision for the truth of God, to confirm the promises made unto the fathers."

—Romans 15:8

IS THE RAPTURE TAUGHT IN MATTHEW 24?

Films on Biblical subjects normally leave much to be desired. In most cases, accuracy is sacrificed on the altar of *misinterpretation* merely to dramatize the events. Over the years, this writer has viewed numerous so-called Christian films only to come away with a sense of disappointment. One particular Old Testament saga depicted the children of Israel crossing the Red Sea knee-deep in water. Here was one of the most remarkable miracles God ever performed being downgraded to a mere natural phenomenon. The Scriptures emphatically declare that the children of Israel crossed through the Red Sea on *dry ground* (Ex. 14:22,29). God miraculously caused the waters to stand up as a heap on the right and on the left and not a single drop of water ever touched His chosen people.

On another occasion, my wife and I were invited to a showing of the film, *"A Thief in the Night."* While producers of the film had good intentions, they missed a golden opportunity to give a clear presentation of the Rapture. After the viewing we were left with the sinking feeling of a wide receiver who drops a fifty yard pass in the end zone. A scoring opportunity was right at his fingertips but he dropped the ball. In like manner, the producer's chance to score a touchdown for the pretribulational Rapture was lost due to a failure to rightly divide the Word of truth.

Perhaps the biggest disappointment in the film came when no distinction was made between the *Secret Coming of Christ* in the Rapture and the *Second Coming* to the earth. The Scriptures concerning these two events were so intermingled it left the viewer with the impression that they were one and the same. Using Matthew Chapter 24 to substantiate their claim of the future Rapture, they quoted the all-familiar passage: "Then shall two be in the field; the one shall be taken, and the other left" (Matt. 24:40). It has been said that, "Necessity is the mother of invention." In this case, it was out of the necessity to produce passages that supposedly teach the Rapture that an erroneous interpretation was applied to this portion. Simply because Matthew 24:36-42 contains a similar concept as I Thessalonians 4 does not imply that the two comings of Christ spoken of in these chapters are identical events. For example, *blue* and *blew* are homonyms, that is, words which sound alike, but have totally *different* meanings. The same is true of these two chapters under consideration.

Before we commence this study, it is imperative to familiarize ourselves with the characteristics of the pretribulational Rapture. As the phrase indicates, the Secret Coming of Christ will *precede* the time of Jacob's trouble.

136

When the trump sounds the Lord will descend into the first heaven, but will be *unseen* by the inhabitants of the earth. Then, the dead in Christ are summoned from their graves in the secret resurrection followed by our translation to glory. Only *believers* are *caught up* into heaven when the Lord returns for the Body of Christ. It is a chilling thought, indeed, that every unbeliever will be left behind to cope with the evil one and experience the undiluted wrath of God. According to the revelation given to the Apostle Paul, the Rapture is an *unprophesied* event, not associated with *signs, times* or *seasons*. Does this, however, coincide with the order of events unfolded in the Olivet discourse?

With God's help, we shall now endeavor to show that the Rapture of the Church is not the theme of Matthew 24.

a. The Olivet Discourse

"And as He sat upon the Mount of Olives, the disciples came unto Him privately, saying, Tell us, when shall these things be? And what shall be the sign of Thy coming, and of the end of the world?" (Matt.24:3).

Prior to this threefold question of the disciples, our Lord had made an unexpected prediction that the day was drawing near when the temple would be destroyed in Jerusalem. We can only imagine the disciples' dismay as the Lord pointed to this magnificent structure and said: "There shall not be left here one stone upon another, that shall not be thrown down."[1]

---

1. Two sieges of Jerusalem are in view — the one took place under Titus in 70 A.D. and the other at the end times. See also Luke 21:20-24.

It is interesting that the twelve identified this prediction with the coming *day of the Lord,* and so should we. Thus, they anxiously inquired, "Tell us when shall these things be? And what shall be the sign of Thy coming and the end of the world?" The answers to these questions are found in what has come to be known as the Olivet discourse. If we were to take the events and ominous warnings of this discourse and lay them next to the master plan of *prophecy,* they match perfectly.

Inasmuch as the theme of prophecy is the millennial kingdom, our Lord announced that during the troublous times that lie ahead the good news of this kingdom will be preached throughout the world (Matt. 24:14). Many will receive hope from this message as they seek to withstand the bloodbath that awaits the world. This explains our Lord's warning to those of that day to flee Jerusalem when they ". . . SEE the abomination of desolation spoken of by the prophet Daniel. . . ." We should point out that a *time* reference is given to us here concerning the Antichrist's rise to power. Therefore, when they *see* the abomination of desolation, which is the man of sin declaring himself to be God, they must immediately flee Jerusalem or risk losing their lives.

Near the close of the Great Tribulation, various *signs* shall appear in heaven which serve as a warning of the Lord's soon return. "Immediately after the tribulation of those days shall the sun be darkened, and the moon shall not give her light, and the stars shall fall from heaven, and the powers of the heavens shall be shaken" (Matt. 24:29). Men's hearts will fail within them as they behold this heavenly exhibition of God's awesome power. As we

138

have noted, the time of Christ's Second Coming could probably be narrowed down to the *day* were it not for a brief *delay* between these *signs in heaven* and the *sign of His coming* in verse 30. In all likelihood, this delay will only be two or three weeks in duration, but it is enough time for the world to dismiss Christ's return in judgment. Life will return to some degree of normalcy as the men lapse back into feasting, drunkenness and immorality. Moreover, two are said to be in the field, and the women will again be grinding at the mill. This is strong evidence that the Second Coming of Christ is going to be an *unexpected* event, which will catch many by surprise as the Lord returns as a thief in the night.

b. The Days of Noah

"But as the days of Noah were, so shall also the coming of the Son of Man be. For as in the days that were before the flood they were eating and drinking, marrying and giving in marriage, until the day that Noah entered into the ark" (Matt. 24:37,38).

When our Lord took His disciples aside and delivered unto them the Olivet discourse, He likened His Second Coming to the days of Noah. This comparison is significant for most are well aware of what transpired in the days leading up to the flood. Violence had filled the earth as men departed from the way of the Lord. So God raised up Noah, who was perfect in his generation to preach against the evils of his day. He persistently warned his generation of the impending judgment to come, but to them his words were as idle tales. They went about fulfilling the desires of the flesh, eating and drinking,

139

marrying and giving in marriage, taking no heed to the warnings of God. Thus, the days of Noah closed with a horrific judgment as the windows of heaven were opened and the fountains of the deep burst forth resulting in a catastrophic, *universal flood* upon the earth.

Please bear with me for a moment, but I must ask an elementary question: Who was removed from the earth in Noah's day—was it the believers or the unbelievers? The Genesis record plainly states that the *unbelievers* were swept away to a watery grave. So shall it be when the Son of Man returns in a flaming fire of vengeance to execute judgment upon His enemies.

> "Then shall two be in the field; the one shall be taken, and the other left. Two women shall be grinding at the mill; the one shall be taken, and the other left" (Matt. 24:40,41).

In conjunction with other Scriptures, there seems to be a subtle hint here that the Second Coming will probably take place in early fall.[2] This, of course, is the *season* when believers and unbelievers alike *harvest* their fields. We learn from the Book of Revelation that near the close of the Great Tribulation, the Antichrist will launch a massive military campaign against God's chosen nation. This is one last attempt to destroy Israel from the face of the earth. As he approaches the valley of Megiddo in northern Palestine, there will undoubtedly be an eerie stillness over the land. Suddenly, the night will turn into day as

---

2. We are cognizant that our Lord used the illustration of the fig tree (springtime) to show the *imminency* of His return *following* the signs in heaven (Luke 21:29-31). But this should not be confused with the underlying teaching that the Second Coming will in all likelihood transpire during the fall (Lev. 23:24 cf. Matt. 13:30).

Christ appears in a blaze of glory with the armies of heaven. "And then shall all the tribes of the earth mourn, and they shall SEE the Son of Man coming in the clouds of heaven with power and great glory" (Matt. 24:30 cf. Rev. 1:7). Like the autumn harvest, these *infidels* will be cut down and cast into outer darkness. On the other hand, the *believers* will remain on the earth as in the days of Noah, to enjoy the blessings of the *kingdom* (Matt. 25:31-46).

Although the parable of the Sower is often interpreted devotionally, it actually sets forth a profound dispensational lesson. As we know, an enemy sowed tares among the wheat in the field of the owner. When the servants found that tares had sprung up with the good seed, they immediately informed their Master. He concluded that an enemy had done this and instructed his servants to "Let both grow together until the *harvest:* and in the time of the harvest I will say to the reapers, Gather ye together first the tares, and bind them in bundles to burn them: but gather the wheat into my barn."

The *harvest* is the end of the age, identified specifically as the battle of Armageddon that will be fought on the plain of Megiddo. Satan is the enemy who successfully deceived the world, represented by the tares. Of course, the reapers are the angels who gather the tares or *unbelievers* at the Second Coming of Christ and cast them into the furnace of fire where there shall be weeping and gnashing of teeth. "Then shall the righteous shine forth as the sun in the kingdom of their Father" (Matt. 13:24-30,36-43).

This conclusion is further substantiated by the very words our Lord chose to use in describing this horrendous event. Here in Matthew 24:40 where it is said "one shall be taken and the other left," the term "taken" is the Greek word *paralambano,* which denotes "to take or lay hold of." This term is frequently associated with *force* and *fury* such as when they *"took* Jesus," stripping Him of His robe and beating Him unmercifully.[3] So, then, in the future day of the Lord, it will be the *unbelievers* in the field and at the mill who are taken by *force* and carried off into perdition.

Who could fail to see that just the *opposite* is true when the translation of the Church takes place. "Then WE [redeemed members of the Body] which are alive and remain shall be caught up together with them in the clouds, to meet the Lord in the air. . ." (I Thes. 4:17). In other words, two shall be sitting at the computer; the one shall be taken, and the other left. Two women shall be shopping at the mall; the one shall be taken, and the other left. Clearly, it is the *believing* members of the Body of Christ who are removed from the earth at the Rapture. "Oh what glory it will be" when we are taken in *peace* and *blessing* to enjoy the riches of His grace for eternity. Hence, Paul was able to reassure us with these words: "Wherefore comfort one another with these words."

A RULE OF THUMB

Is the Rapture taught in Matthew 24? To this, we reply with an emphatic—NO! Perhaps this rule of thumb will be helpful in distinguishing between the two comings of Christ. The Scriptures that precede and follow the

---

3. See E. W. Vine's *Expository Dictionary of Old and New Testament Words*—Pages 104,105.

Pauline epistles *promise, teach* and *confirm* the Second Coming of Christ to the earth. Only in Paul's letters do we find the Secret Coming of Christ, commonly known as the *Rapture.* If this rule of thumb is applied consistently, it will take the fog out of our teaching on the *two* returns of Christ promised in the Word of God. May God use this feeble effort to His glory to underscore the importance of rightly dividing the Word of truth.

IS THE RAPTURE TAUGHT IN JOHN 14?

When *tradition* speaks, most Christians bow in humble adoration without regard to the Word, rightly divided. A case in point is the dispensational position that the Rapture is taught in John Chapter 14. Dr. Harry Ironside is one of the voices from the past who adequately expressed the *traditional view* that many believers still follow today: "When the Lord Jesus fulfills that which is spoken here in the fourteenth chapter of John, then believers [the Body of Christ] will receive their glorified bodies and will be altogether like Him. This coming [Rapture], referred to here, is developed for us more fully in the fourth chapter of First Thessalonians."[4] After Dr. Ironside cites I Thessalonians 4:13-18, he goes on to quote from Romans and Philippians to further substantiate his claim.

One of the rules of hermeneutics (science of interpretation) states: Your conclusion is only as sound as your premise. In other words, if your premise is incorrect, your conclusion, as convincing as it may be, is also *wrong.* Dr. Ironside concludes that the Rapture is taught in John 14 on the basis that our Lord gave to His disciples a special

----

4. *The Gospel of John* by H. A. Ironside—Pp. 597,598.

revelation on the matter. However, a proper understanding of the *Mystery* reveals that the truth of the Rapture was a secret hidden in God until made known to the Apostle Paul. This signifies that the additional light our Lord gave His disciples that fateful night must be interpreted in accordance with the *Prophetic program.*

a. The Gospel According to John

Because the Apostle John wrote his gospel long after the death of the Apostle Paul, some have drawn the conclusion that since he had a knowledge of Paul's gospel it was only natural for him to embrace it. It is true, of course, that John was keenly aware of the new revelation committed to the apostle of the Gentiles, but this does not necessarily imply that he incorporated it into his writings. This would only serve to confuse the two programs of God. We believe that even though John acknowledged the fall of Israel, he remained consistent with the *kingdom gospel* of which he was an apostle.

Suppose for a moment that you are 87 years old. Having learned of your longevity, a publisher approaches you to write an autobiography about the *Life and Times of World War II.* Although you have a knowledge of the *Korean Conflict, Vietnam* and *Desert Storm,* you must confine your thoughts to the era of the Second World War. In like manner, the Holy Spirit moved John to only chronicle the *earthly ministry* of Christ of which he had firsthand knowledge. Thus, John remains consistent with the Prophetic theme as demonstrated in John 20:31:

> "But these [the events of the life of Christ] are written, that ye [Hebrews] might believe that Jesus is the

Christ [Messiah of Israel], the Son of God; and that believing ye might have life through His name."

The gospel according to John is inseparably linked to the *kingdom gospel* and, therefore, is addressed to the nation Israel. Interestingly, the terminology practically leaps off the page as *every* reference to titles, events and places is directly associated with the law and the prophets. Perhaps a few examples are in order:

"And this is the record of John, when the JEWS sent PRIESTS and LEVITES from JERUSALEM to ask him, Who art thou?" (John 1:19).

"And I knew Him not: but that He [Messiah] should be made manifest to ISRAEL, therefore am I come baptizing with water" (John 1:31).

"Nathanael answered and saith unto Him, RABBI, Thou art the Son of God; Thou art the KING OF ISRAEL" (John 1:49).

"And the JEWS' PASSOVER was at hand, and Jesus went up to JERUSALEM, and found in the TEMPLE. . ." (John 2:13,14).

"Ye worship ye know not what: we know what we worship: for SALVATION IS OF THE JEWS" (John 4:22).

b. Troubled Hearts

"Let not your heart be troubled: ye believe in God, believe also in me" (John 14:1).

In the shadow of Calvary, our Lord gathered His disciples in the upper room that they might partake of the *last supper.* After the meal, the Master made a startling prediction that one of them would *betray* Him. As silence filled the room the disciples turned and looked at each

145

other wondering who among them would stoop to such a cowardly deed. It was one of those soul-searching moments when each disciple, acutely aware of his own weakness, pondered the unthinkable: "Is it I Lord?" Little wonder their hearts were *troubled;* they were distraught that one among them would betray the Master (John 13:21-30).

Following the announcement of His betrayal, our Lord had to give the disciples another piece of distressing news. The hour of His crucifixion was at hand; consequently, He would soon have to leave them, but where He was going they would be unable to follow. As they contemplated His words, many concerns arose in their hearts. Peter stepped forward to inquire, "Lord, whither goest thou?" Of course, the Lord was going to return to heaven by way of the Cross. The thought of the Master's departure had an unsettling effect upon the disciples; so much so, that Peter declared that he would be willing to fight to the death to defend Him. This is another example that the apostles did not understand the significance of the death of Christ. The Lord slowly turned to Peter and said, "Verily, verily, I say unto thee, The cock shall not crow, till thou hast denied me thrice" (John 13:33-38).

This turn of events explains why the hearts of the disciples were *troubled,* and why it was necessary for the Lord to console them before His return to His heavenly Father.

c. The Father's House

"In my Father's house are many mansions: if it were not so, I would have told you. I go to prepare a place for you" (John 14:2).

Generally these passages are taken to mean that our Lord returned to His Father's house in heaven where He donned a carpenter's apron for the sole purpose of building mansions for us in the heavenlies. Upon completion, He will return for the Body of Christ in the Rapture, at which time we will take possession of our beautiful, spacious mansions in the sky. Now, this sounds positively romantic; however, this is the voice of tradition and not the *sound* teaching of the Word of God!

According to the Scriptures, the *Father's house* is a reference to the *temple* in Jerusalem (John 2:13-17). Inasmuch as the Lord connects this promise with His Second Coming back to the earth, we are to conclude that the *millennial temple* spoken of by Ezekiel is in view (Ezek. 43:1-7). Thus, when Christ returns in glory to redeem Israel, one of His first undertakings will be to rebuild the temple in Jerusalem. When the structure is restored to its original magnificence, then the Son of Man will sit on the throne of His glory. In the millennial temple there will be "many mansions." The particular Greek word used here by John is *"Mone"* which simply denotes "an abiding place." Like the temples of old, Ezekiel teaches us that there will be *living quarters* for the priests and Levites who minister in the things of God (Ezek. 40). In the upper room discourse, this promise is extended to the disciples, which gives us further insight into the statement: ". . . where I am, there ye may be also."

It must have been music to their ears when they learned that the Lord would come again. In addition, not only shall they reign with Christ on 12 thrones judging the 12 tribes of Israel, they shall also have the privilege of

147

residing at the temple. It does seem doubtful though that this promise was intended for all the kingdom saints. Be that as it may, the disciples were comforted by the fact that they would one day be reunited with their blessed Lord.

"I go to prepare a place for you" should be understood in light of the parable of the ten pounds. "He said therefore, A certain nobleman went into a far country to receive for himself a kingdom, and to return. And he called his ten servants, and delivered them ten pounds, and said unto them, Occupy till I come" (Luke 19:12,13). The nobleman is Christ, who returns to heaven so that He might receive the *kingdom* from His heavenly Father. In His absence, believing Israel will be observed to determine whether or not they have been trustworthy in carrying out the *Great Commission.* Their position, authority and rewards in the kingdom age will depend upon their faithfulness to that which is recorded in the four Gospels. So then, the placement of those who enter into the *times of refreshing,* including the disciples, will be contingent on how they conduct themselves in the Messiah's absence.

COMING AGAIN

"And if I go and prepare a place for you, I will come again, and receive you unto myself; that where I am, there ye may be also" (John 14:3).

While the disciples were sorting out why the Lord must leave them at this time, the Prophetic Scriptures set forth no less than four reasons for His departure. First, the Savior must die for the sins of His people (Israel) and appear in heaven before His Father as the *Lamb of God* (Isa. 53:3-11; Luke 2:11,36-38; John 20:17 cf. Rev. 5:8-10). Second, according to prophecy Christ must be seated

148

at the right hand of the Father in heaven until all His enemies are made His footstool (Psa. 110:1 cf. Acts 2:32-36).
Third, as mentioned earlier, in His royal exile Christ will
receive the kingdom from His Father that had been
promised since the foundation of the world (Luke 19:12 cf.
Matt. 25:31-34). Finally, with the King in exile, the kingdom saints will be *tested* as they are called upon to endure
the dreaded tribulation period (Zeph. 1:14,15 cf. Luke
19:11-27).

The consolation of the disciples, indeed of all believing
Israelites, is nestled in the words: "I will come again."
There is no question that we have before us a clear reference to the *Second Coming* of Christ. The matter is set-
tled by simply asking—where was Christ when He spoke
these words to His disciples? He was seated in the upper
room ON THE EARTH! When the Son of Man returns in
His glory He will literally stand on the Mount of Olives,
probably not far from the dimly lit room where they ate
the last supper (Job 19:15-27; Zech. 14:4).

Upon His return to Jerusalem, Christ will overthrow
the kingdoms of the world and establish His kingdom of
righteousness for one *thousand years*. One of the first
matters of business will be the reconstruction of the *temple* prophesied by Ezekiel. It could well be our Lord will
merely speak it into existence with the Word of His power.
From this newly established seat of authority, Christ will
judge Israel and the nations. At this point in time, three
promises are fulfilled that were made with the disciples
during the earthly ministry of Christ:

1. "Verily I say unto you [the 12], That ye which have
followed me, in the regeneration [re-creation—millennial

149

kingdom] when the Son of Man shall sit in the throne of His glory, ye also shall sit upon twelve thrones, judging the twelve tribes of Israel."

2. "In my Father's house are many mansions...." The apostles will occupy the "abodes" promised them in the upper room, which is one of the rewards of their inheritance. They will finally receive that long-awaited millennial rest.

3. "I will come again, and receive you unto myself; that where I am, there ye may be also." Full access! What we enjoy now by grace, Israel will one day rejoice in as well. The apostles shall never again be separated from the Lord who loved them and gave Himself for them.

A SUPPLEMENTARY WORD

Of course, with the temporary abandonment of God's program of prophecy, He is making known the riches of His grace to undeserving sinners like you and me. Today, then, we are under grace whereby God is carrying out His *secret purpose* for the Church the Body of Christ. Insofar as the doctrines of grace are solely limited to the Mystery program, it can only mean that the Rapture must *first* take place before God will resume His Prophetic program.

Those who teach that the Rapture is expounded in Matthew 24 or John 14 often find that those who sit under their ministry drift off into a mid- or posttribulational position. This should not surprise us since both of these contexts deal exclusively with the *day of the Lord*. The antidote to avoid falling prey to this type of error is found, once again, in a knowledge of the Word, *rightly divided*. It

150

is well worth repeating that when our Lord uttered these words to His disciples in John Chapter 14, the Rapture was yet a SECRET hidden in the mind of God.

As we know, tradition nearly had a deathgrip on the Church preceding the great *Reformation*. The only force that had enough power to cancel its unyielding grasp was the living Word of God. Needless to say, the voice of tradition still holds almost unbelievable sway over many dear saints. To be freed from its shackles, we plead with you to study all Scripture in light of Paul's epistles for the truth will be vindicated at the Judgment Seat of Christ. As Isaiah the prophet said many years ago, "Come let us reason together" that we may all make the *truth* known as co-laborers with Christ! AMEN!

9

Our Lord's Resurrection

"But now is Christ risen from the dead, and become the firstfruits of them that slept. For since by man came death, by man came also the resurrection of the dead."

—*I Corinthians 15:20,21*

Americans pride themselves on the fact that the United States Constitution guarantees each citizen the right to a trial by jury. In other words, we can all have our day in court. Hence, our judicial system has served us well for the past two hundred years. Using it as a model, we would like you, the "heavenly citizen," to judge as to the certainty of our Lord's *resurrection.* Through the years, the Modernists have gone to great lengths to mount a foolproof case against the resurrection of Christ. They not only deny His resurrection but have sought to explain it away with sweeping statements, thus questioning the accuracy of God's Word. This writer would like the reader to be the judge and jury in this case as we present the evidence provided in the Scriptures. The verdict is yours though the truth will remain the same!

EVIDENCE FROM THE GRAVE CLOTHES

We begin our case by presenting the evidence from the grave clothes as recorded in the gospel according to John.

153

> "And there came also Nicodemus . . . and brought a mixture of myrrh and aloes, about an hundred pound weight. Then took they the body of Jesus, and wound it in linen clothes with the spices, as the manner of the Jews is to bury" (John 19:39,40).

The manner of the Jewish burial was to first prepare the body in the customary way and then bury the deceased the same day that death occurred. The procedure began by first washing the body with warm water and then dressing all the wounds. You will remember when Dorcas died this practice was followed when they washed her and laid her in the upper chamber (Acts 9:36,37). These washings were unquestionably connected to the ceremonial baptisms of the law (Hebrews 9:10).

Having washed the body, they proceeded to mix the myrrh and aloes together which created a type of pasty substance (aloes was fragments of wood, pulverized into dust and mixed with myrrh, which was used as perfume). Next, the body was wrapped from under the arms to the feet applying the mixture of myrrh and aloes as the body was wound. This formed approximately a 120 pound encasement around the corpse. Undoubtedly, Joseph and Nicodemus performed this procedure either very near or even possibly inside the tomb that the Lord would be buried. This would have brought the weight of the corpse to approximately 300 pounds. Finally, they placed a napkin under the chin and tied it at the top of the head to hold the jaw of the Master in place. The stone was then rolled in front of the entrance, sealed with the Roman seal, and a watch was placed at the request of the Chief Priest.

154

On resurrection morning, Mary Magdalene arrived early at the tomb, and to her amazement she saw that the stone had been moved and the body of our Lord was gone (John 20:1-10). She promptly found Peter and John and declared to them all that she had seen. Astonished, Peter and John raced to the tomb, John outrunning Peter, perhaps because he was the younger of the two. Or could it have been that Peter was guilt-ridden because he had denied his Master?

Arriving first at the sepulcher, John stooped down, ". . . and looking in, *saw* the linen clothes lying; yet went he not in" (Ver. 5). The word "saw" used here by the Spirit is the Greek word "BLEPO," which means merely to glance at something. Have you ever gone through a traffic light and just glanced at it, not paying very close attention? Looking back in the rear view mirror, with a sigh of relief you're thankful that your subconscious served you well because the light was indeed green. John had a similar experience when he just glanced in and thought, "He's gone!" not really giving the matter in-depth thought.

Next, Peter came running in a cloud of dust (forgetting his ceremonial separation from the dead according to the law), and entered the tomb, ". . . and *seeth* the linen clothes lie" (Ver. 6). The word "seeth" in the original language is "THEOREO," from which we get our English word, theory. The word John uses here means to look in amazement at something. A good example of this is when the shuttle *Challenger* exploded on January 28, 1986 over Cape Canaveral. When we first saw the film footage of the disaster we looked in amazement, we couldn't believe what we were seeing! We watched with great interest

155

while at the same time questioning what had happened. With this in mind, we can better appreciate how Peter gazed into the empty sepulcher and was dumbfounded as he beheld the grave clothes lying there like an empty cocoon. When Christ had risen from the dead, He had come out of the encasement of grave clothes *supernaturally,* without disturbing any of the wrappings. Peter was overwhelmed at the sight and wondered what could have happened.

The scene now changes back to John, as he stepped back into the doorway, ". . . and he *saw,* and believed" (Ver. 8). The word "saw" in this passage is the Greek "EIDON," which conveys the thought that he saw for the first time with *perception.* Remember back in Senior High School, when you agonized over a difficult algebra problem? You wondered if that equation could ever be solved in this lifetime. Just about that time, the teacher came by giving you a suggestion and suddenly it dawned on you— you saw, or perceived, how to solve the problem. John was the first to perceive that the reason the tomb was empty and the grave clothes left behind was because Christ had *risen* from the dead!

Those who reject the truth of the resurrection of Christ seek to explain it away by saying, "Christ never died on the Cross, but was simply unconscious and upon being placed into the cool tomb, He revived." This is preposterous for a number of reasons. First of all, the Romans and the Jews were both authorities when it came to pronouncing one dead, the Romans especially being masters of the art (John 19:32-35). To show how absurd this theory is, we are asked to believe, *humanly speaking,* that like a trick by Houdini, Christ somehow slipped out of the grave clothes that was like a concrete cast around His body. Following that mighty achievement, He took the time to reconstruct the shell of the grave clothes that was originally placed on His body. He then folded the napkin that was about His head and laid it at the head of the resting place. Being near the point of exhaustion, He somehow rolled the massive stone, weighing over a ton, away from the entrance. He then overcame the Roman guards who were trained in battle and whose lives were at stake to protect that with which they had been entrusted. Finally, Christ escaped into the night unnoticed.

This would have been nearly as great a miracle as the resurrection itself! The evidence of the *empty tomb* and the grave clothes declares beyond a shadow of a doubt: Christ *did* rise from the dead! Members of the jury, the evidence clearly points to *the bodily resurrection of Jesus Christ!*

EVIDENCE FROM THE CIRCUMSTANCES

The next area of testimony comes to us from the circumstances surrounding resurrection morning. The Chief Priest and the Pharisees had requested of Pilate that the sepulcher be made sure, due to the fact that Christ had predicted He would rise again the third day. They feared that the disciples would come by night and steal the body, thus claiming the fulfillment of His words (Matthew 27:62-64). Pilate granted their petition, sealing the tomb and setting a watch (Matthew 27:65,66). The prestigious Roman seal placed on the tomb *guaranteed* that Christ's body was actually there. And you can be sure that the

157

guards who were put in charge would have borne witness to the fact that the body of Jesus was in the tomb before it was sealed. Bear in mind, their lives depended on that body being in that tomb if inspected. Naturally, they would have demanded to see it to make sure it was there in the first place. The "watch," in such a significant matter as this, would probably have consisted of a band of 16 soldiers. Four soldiers would guard the entrance of the tomb at all times and be relieved at the end of their watch by another squadron of four that usually camped nearby. The rotation would have continued through the four watches of the night.

Early on resurrection morning, which was the first day of the week, during the fourth watch an angel appeared and rolled the stone from the entrance (Matthew 28:2-4). The keepers were frozen in their tracks for fear of him that sat on the stone. After seeing that the tomb was empty, visibly shaken, they fled for their lives. The angel invited Mary Magdalene and the other Mary to come see where the Lord lay. From this point, word spread quickly that the tomb was empty and Christ was risen from the dead!

When some of the watch (indicating there were more than two soldiers) came into the city, they disclosed all they had seen and heard unto the Chief Priest. The assembly of the elders bribed the soldiers to take large sums of money to alter their story (Matthew 28:11,12). They were persuaded to do so because if word came to the governor's ears that they had lost custody of a dead man they would have been immediately put to death. Promising them security, the elders persuaded the soldiers

158

to say, ". . . His disciples came by night, and stole Him away while we slept" (Ver. 13). This saying was commonly reported among the Jews years after the resurrection and it remains a favorite tale of some unbelievers today. Members of the jury, be it known that these charges cannot be substantiated and are false! Let's begin by cross-examining the soldiers who stood by the tomb in the wee hours of the morning. If the soldiers were asleep on their watch, as it is claimed they were, then I must ask, "How did they know it was the disciples who stole Him from His resting place?" It would be impossible for them to know this for certain if they were asleep! Futhermore, these soldiers who were trained in battle are asking us to believe that the disciples came by night and *stole* the body.

Picture this scenario, at *least* four disciples came under the cover of darkness to the sepulcher. They passed 12 sleeping soldiers in camp without waking anyone. At the tomb, they broke the seal on the entrance without making a sound. They remarkably rolled the one-ton stone away from the door without awakening the four guards stationed there who were supposedly dozing. They entered the tomb, unwrapped the body, and neatly folded and rearranged the grave clothes. Then, they bore the corpse passed all the soldiers without causing any of them to stir out of their slumber.

I don't know about you, but it takes more faith to believe that than to believe in the resurrection itself! The evidence from the *circumstances* unquestionably points to the resurrection of Christ from the dead that glorious morning!

159

EVIDENCE FROM THE EYEWITNESS ACCOUNTS

One of the strongest cases an attorney can put together is to have eyewitness accounts by those who were present at the scene. The evidence from *eyewitness* accounts of the resurrection of Christ is *insurmountable*. The Apostle Paul gives us an impressive list of those who saw Christ alive after His resurrection.

> "And . . . He was seen of Cephas, then of the twelve: After that, He was seen of above five hundred brethren at once: of whom the greater part remain unto this present, but some are fallen asleep. After that, He was seen of James; then of all the apostles. And last of all He was seen of me also. . ." (I Corinthians 15:5-8).

Paul is careful to document the fact that the resurrected Christ was seen by different people, at different places, at different times. The Scriptures reveal that the Lord showed Himself alive to Mary Magdalene in the garden early on resurrection morning (John 20:14-18). He then appeared to the women returning to tell the disciples of what they had seen and heard (Matthew 28:5-10). It is interesting that Paul does not mention these first two eyewitness accounts of the women. In that day, testimony of women would have been inadmissable as evidence because they were considered in such low esteem. The apostle begins with Peter, who would be the first credible witness, whose testimony would be accepted (Luke 24:34).

He then declares that the twelve saw Christ in His resurrection form. Here, Paul apparently combines the first two appearances of Christ to the disciples (John 20:19-29). A short time later, the Lord was seen by five hundred

160

brethren at once in Galilee (Matthew 28:10,16). Paul says of these five hundred, ". . . the greater part remain unto this present. . . ." In essence he is saying, "If you don't believe me that Christ rose again from the dead, some of these five hundred brethren are yet alive and will bear witness to the truth of His resurrection."

To show you the magnitude of this body of evidence, let's suppose for a moment you are among a group of five hundred people standing across the street from the First National Bank. Suddenly, the burglar alarm is tripped, indicating a bank robbery is in progress. The bank robber comes bursting out of the front doors and comes face to face with five hundred bystanders who have turned around to see what all the commotion was about. A short time later, the robber is apprehended and brought to trial. Those of the witnesses who can be located—say 320 of them—are summoned and all identify the man as the one who had robbed the bank. That robber doesn't have a hope or a prayer of escaping justice! It is inevitable that he will be convicted of the crime and sentenced accordingly. The five hundred eyewitnesses of the resurrected Christ certainly provide inescapable evidence to its *reality*.

Next, Christ was seen of James who was the half brother of our Lord (Matthew 13:55). This was followed by another visitation of Christ to all of the apostles, undoubtedly by the Sea of Galilee (John 21:1,14). Finally, the glorified, resurrected Christ appeared to Paul on the road to Damascus. Some of the most convincing proofs of the resurrection of Christ come to us from James and Paul. The early appearances of Christ were made exclusively to believers—Cephas, the twelve and the five hundred brethren. But in the case of James and Paul, they were yet in unbelief and were both converted to Christ as a result of His resurrection. In Paul's case, his conversion was a direct outcome of Christ's appearance to him on the road to Damascus.

Members of the jury, I rest my case. The evidence I have set forth demands a verdict. The only conclusion we can arrive at with such voluminous evidence and such reliable witnesses is that Christ has indeed risen from the dead! To listen to the skeptic, the agnostic or the liberal is like putting the foxes in charge of the henhouse; the truth will be lost. The importance of the fact of the resurrection of Christ cannot be overstated for this reason:

". . . IF CHRIST BE NOT RAISED, YOUR FAITH IS VAIN; YE ARE YET IN YOUR SINS" (I Cor. 15:17).

10

The Order of the Resurrections

"For as in Adam all die, even so in Christ shall all be made alive. But every man in his own order: Christ the firstfruits; afterward they that are Christ's at His coming."

—*I Corinthians 15:22,23*

THE RESURRECTION OF THE BODY

A short time ago, I was downstairs at the *Berean Bible Society* dictating a letter when a church bell unexpectedly broke my train of thought. Since it was only ten minutes past eleven, I commented to my secretary that it seemed like such an unusual time to be ringing a bell, although it was a pleasant sound replacing the normal deafening roar of aircraft overhead. Pleasant, that is, until I found out its purpose. Rosemary replied—she's always on top of everything—"the bell was to notify the community that someone's funeral was taking place." The incident brought to mind the old English preacher who captured the attention of his congregation when he said, "Some day my friend, the bell that tolls, will toll for thee!" What a startling reminder that death is stalking each of us.

However, in the famous words of Paul Harvey, "Now for the rest of the story. . . ." Believers need not fear death for we sorrow not as others who have no hope. Christ has drawn back the curtain of death, having conquered the

163

enemy by rising victoriously over it *forevermore*. Therefore, He has removed the sting of death, causing it no longer to be the king of terrors. As the first tulip in the spring indicates, there are more soon to follow. When Christ arose from the dead, it was the *guarantee* of our *future resurrection*.

a. The Nature of the Resurrection

"But some man will say, How are the dead raised up? and with what body do they come?" (I Cor. 15:35).

Cynicism ran deep at Corinth which explains why these two questions were posed before Paul. While the Greek philosophers argued for the immortality of the soul, they believed that the resurrection of the body was *preposterous*. The more things change, the more they seem to remain the same. Objections to the resurrection today still range from the sincere inquiry to the absurd.

Some inquire as to how it is possible for the body to be reconstructed after it has turned to dust. Critics attempt to complicate the matter by pointing to accounts of genocide throughout history where hundreds and sometimes even thousands of bodies were buried in mass graves. Then there are those who openly defy God by having their ashes scattered from a plane. Of course, they conclude that by having their remains strewn over twenty square miles they will never be found. Needless to say, they are in for a rude awakening on two fronts: First, *nothing* is impossible with God. Second, according to the Scriptures, God's creation is a *closed system*.

The *First Law of Thermodynamics,* commonly known as the *Law of Conservation and Mass Energy,* plainly states

164

that nothing is being *created* or *annihilated* in the universe. Nehemiah writes: "Thou, even Thou, art Lord alone; Thou hast made heaven, the heaven of heavens, with all their host, the earth, and all things that are therein, the seas, and all that is therein, and Thou PRESERVEST THEM ALL; and the host of heaven worshippeth Thee" (Neh. 9:6). In other words, God is preserving all things; consequently, nothing in creation can ever be removed from His presence. The *form of matter* can be changed, but it is impossible to take its basic molecular structure out of existence. For example, from the small acorn springs forth the mighty oak tree that towers heavenward. If the oak is cut down to produce lumber for making furniture, the tree has taken on a *new* form but it remains in existence. Moreover, if the factory that is building the furniture burns to the ground, amidst the rubble are the ashes of the mighty oak. Remarkably, Job taught the *First Law of Thermodynamics* centuries before it became known as such.

> "For I know that my Redeemer liveth, and that He shall stand at the latter day upon the earth: And though after my skin worms destroy this body [physical body], yet in my flesh [Job's resurrected body] shall I see God" (Job 19:25,26).

Job had the confident expectation that even though death would rob him of life, he would rise again to stand with his Redeemer on Mount Zion. It will be a small matter for God to gather up the dust of our frame, which has been *preserved,* and call us forth in the resurrection. Did not God create man from the dust of the earth in the beginning?

The Apostle Paul sternly answers those who were skeptical of the resurrection with these words: "Thou fool, that which thou sowest is not quickened, except it die" (I Cor. 15:36). He challenges them to study the world of nature, for in so doing the resurrection is indisputable. To deny its existence is to deny springtime and the harvest.

Having established the fact of the resurrection, *how shall we appear in glory?*

b. The Identity Crisis

"And that which thou sowest, thou sowest not that body that shall be, but bare grain, it may chance of wheat, or of some other grain: But God giveth it a body as it hath pleased Him, and to every seed his own body" (I Cor. 15:37,38).

Here the apostle draws an illustration from the realm of agriculture. If you take a kernel of corn and plant it in a furrow, it must first die and begin to decay before a sprout of life issues forth. From that small kernel of corn comes the stalk which bears the ears of corn. The same body but in a different form which is similar to another phenomenon in nature known as *metamorphosis.* This is the physical transformation that takes place when the caterpillar turns into a beautiful butterfly. So it shall be in the resurrection! These vile bodies of humiliation given to corruption and weakness will be *changed* into glorified, resurrected bodies. We will be raised incorruptible—no more pain, sickness, sorrow or death.

But there is more: Paul is also teaching us by way of this illustration that our *identity* will be preserved. In that tiny kernel of corn, God has programmed everything that we have come to know that is characteristic of corn.

166

Thus, when it is planted we do not expect to harvest cauliflower, but *corn*. When the Body of Christ is raised from the dead at the Rapture, we shall be known even as we are presently known, sin excluded. In the Book of Philippians, it is recorded that our bodies will be ". . . fashioned like unto His glorious body."

The day that Christ arose, He appeared that evening to His disciples in the upper room. The Scriptures teach us that they were terrified at His presence, supposing that they had seen a spirit. The disciples who were present that night are sometimes chided for their lack of faith. However, I would venture to say that if the Lord were to pass through the wall in the room where we were sitting probably most of us would need to be resuscitated. To calm the fears of the disciples, our Lord uttered these words, "Peace be unto you." In all probability, they turned and looked at one another in amazement. They first recognized the sound of His voice. How could they fail not to—it was a voice that they had listened to every day for nearly three and one-half years. Now they were hearing it again from one who had walked through the valley of the shadow of death. Could it be that He has risen as he said He would?

Next the Master said, "Behold my hands and my feet, that it is I myself." His *identity* was preserved in the resurrection. Everyone has had the experience of observing the facial expression of someone who has been totally surprised; it's one of the memorable moments in life. Imagine the disciples' stare of disbelief when they beheld the nailprints in the Savior's hands and feet. The words of Thomas on another occasion sum it up well: "My Lord

167

and My God." Although blemishes will probably be uncharacteristic of our resurrected bodies, the *scars* of our Lord's crucifixion will be a constant reminder throughout eternity that Christ died for our sins (Luke 24:33-41; John 20:24-29).

Returning to the Prophetic program for a moment, our Lord makes a significant statement that further substantiates the foregoing conclusion. "And I say unto you, That many shall come from the east and west, and shall sit down with Abraham, and Isaac, and Jacob, in the kingdom of heaven" (Matt. 8:11). If this is true, then it will be necessary that the *identity* of these three patriarchs be *preserved* when they are raised in the first resurrection preceding the kingdom. Indeed, there will be *recognition* both in the earthly and heavenly realms of the kingdom of God.

c. The Results of Being Changed

"There are also celestial bodies, and bodies terrestrial: but the glory of the celestial is one, and the glory of the terrestrial is another" (I Cor. 15:40).

The Word of God teaches us that there will be different degrees of glorification in the resurrection based on the faithfulness of the believer (Heb. 11:35). Our faithfulness not only has a bearing on our reigning position with Christ; it will also determine the degree to which our bodies will be glorified. This is the basis of Paul's argument in I Corinthians 15:40,41 concerning the celestial bodies. There are diversities of glory in the heavens. The sun has a greater light than that of the moon. Thus, the sun has a greater glory than the moon. On the other hand, the moon has a greater glory than the stars, yet one star differeth from another in glory. *"So also is the resurrection of the dead."*

168

"It is sown in corruption; it is raised in incorruption" (I Cor. 15:42).

The best teacher always serves as a guide as demonstrated by the Apostle Paul who moves on to effectively show the contrast between our natural and spiritual bodies. For years, medical science has known that our bodies are constantly reproducing new cells which means we should live forever. However, what has baffled them to the point of distraction is the fact that in spite of this we age and eventually die. The answer is really quite simple, *we are sown in corruption.* Every Egyptian mummy that has ever been unearthed stands as a solemn reminder of this fundamental truth.

At God's appointed time, He is going to raise these bodies of humiliation, clothing us with our house which is *eternal* in the heavens. This means with the abolition of the curse our glorified bodies will be *imperishable.* Blood will not sustain our existence in eternity; rather, it will be the Spirit who energizes our new tabernacle. The results of this will be phenomenal—all believers will enjoy perfect sight, perfect hearing and have an endless source of energy. We will no longer suffer from anxious moments, loneliness, despair, *et al.*

"It is sown in dishonor; it is raised in glory. . ." (I Cor. 15:43).

It should be self-evident that the natural body is *sown in dishonor* because of the fall of Adam. The *New England Primer* hits the nail on the head:

> In Adam's fall
> We sinned all
>
> Xerxes the Great did die
> And so must you and I.

Some of the more common ways men dishonor themselves and God are rebellion, unbelief, drug abuse, alcoholism, child abuse, immorality, filthy language, etc. Yes, even believers sometimes indulge in things they ought not do but, thankfully, a day of deliverance is coming.

The other side of dishonor is *glory*. When stamped in the image of the heavenly, *all believers* will possess the *mind of Christ*. Every thought, word and deed will be in perfect harmony with the will of God. We will be glorified in Him and He in us. May our prayer be: Teach us oh Lord, to number our days and apply our hearts in wisdom, that we may enjoy the *full benefit* of that which You have made available for us.

> "It is sown in weakness; it is raised in power"
> (I Cor. 15:43).

About ten years ago, I came to a fuller appreciation of this passage. With a growing ministry, I found myself taking on more and more responsibilities in the Lord's work. Eventually, this staggering schedule put me flat on my back in a hospital intensive care unit with *hypertension*. After two weeks of recuperation, it was all I could do to muster enough strength to walk across the room. I never realized how weak one could become until that unsettling experience. During my convalescing, the above passage kept flashing across my mind. When you are bedridden and it takes a major effort to lift your arm, believe me it's *good news* that someday soon we are going to be raised in *power.*

170

Thankfully, our resurrected bodies will not be subject to weakness nor be limited to space. Natural laws, such as gravity, will in no way hinder our ability to move freely in heavenly realms. We will have a continuous source of strength enabling us to serve our blessed Lord throughout eternity.

What a wonderful hope we have as believers in the resurrection of the dead! Death has no claims on us—we have *victory* through Christ Jesus our Lord and the hope of everlasting life.

But what is the significance of the resurrection in our Christian walk? Death is an enemy that separates us from those we love. But the hope of the resurrection ensures that we shall *see* them again. Someday, death will rob you of a loved one, but this wonderful truth will enable you to endure the terrible sense of loss. There may also come that day when the physician points to an X-ray and says, "I'm sorry, but your condition is terminal." The hope of the resurrection will help you weather the storm. In addition, the power of Christ's resurrection is at our disposal, thus enabling us to triumph over extenuating circumstances to the praise of His glory (Phil. 3:10).

THE ORDER OF THE RESURRECTIONS

"For since by man came death, by man came also the resurrection of the dead. For as in Adam all die, even so in Christ shall all be made alive" (I Cor. 15:21,22).

Those who fail to rightly divide the Word of truth find themselves in quite a dilemma when it comes to the *order of the resurrections.* Even the highly-esteemed Dr.

171

Scofield floundered around when approaching this topic. Commenting on the resurrection of the Body of Christ at the Rapture in I Thessalonians 4:13-17, he wrote: "Not Church saints only, but all bodies of the saved, of whatever dispensation, are included in the first resurrection (see I Cor. 15:52 note), as here described, but it is peculiarly the "blessed hope" of the Church (cf. Matt. 24:42; 25:13; Luke 12:36-48; Acts 1:11; Phil. 3:20,21; Titus 2:11-13)."[1]

If the resurrection that Paul taught is the first resurrection as Dr. Scofield claims, then how can the resurrection which follows seven years later be called the first resurrection? (Rev. 20:6). Obviously, this interpretation has been weighed in the balance and found wanting. The solution to the problem, once again, is found in the proper division of God's Word.

a. The Prophetic Order

"But every man in his own order: Christ the firstfruits; afterward they that are Christ's at His coming" (I Cor. 15:23).

Assuming that we understand that the major division in the Word of God is between Prophecy and the Mystery, in verses 23-28 the apostle introduces us to the *Prophetic order* of the future resurrections. *"But every man in his own order. . . ."* This particular passage refutes a general resurrection in that the word "order" is a military term which is used to describe *different* companies of soldiers. Paul, of course, was not a military man himself, but he was quite familiar with the procedures of the Roman army. After all, he had been a prisoner of Rome for a number of years.

---

1. The *Scofield Reference Bible,* C. I Scofield, Page 1269.

We can just picture the great apostle looking out of a window as a regiment of soldiers marched by. Upon inquiring as to their destination, he is informed by one of the guards that they have been commissioned to rule over a certain city in the name of Caesar. A short time later, *another* battalion of soldiers marches past. This time, however, Paul is told that the Emperor is displeased with this company so they are being sent to the front lines of a raging battle—sure death awaits them! Similarly, there will be *different companies* who will march forth from the grave at God's appointed time—some to everlasting life and others to everlasting condemnation!

The Scriptures declare that Christ is the firstfruits from the dead; the firstfruits, implying that which precedes the main harvest. They are the first to ripen and, therefore, are a foretaste of what is to come. Although there have been numerous resuscitations of those who have grappled with death, Christ was the first to conquer it by rising victoriously over this formidable foe. Thus, His bodily resurrection *guarantees* the great harvest that is yet to come.

Paul effectively shows us how the first company that comes forth in the *Prophetic* order will be, ". . . *they* that are Christ's at His coming" (Vs. 23). Carefully note that it is not "we" that are Christ's at His coming, but rather "they." This is unquestionably a reference to Israel and the other prophetic saints who possess an earthly hope. When Christ returns in His Second Coming at the close of the Great Tribulation, He will raise these saints from the dead for the sole purpose of ushering them into His earthly kingdom.

According to the Prophetic program, then, this is the *first resurrection,* oftentimes referred to as the resurrection to everlasting life, and includes all of the saved from the former prophetic dispensations. Moreover, those believers who die during the future tribulation period will also be numbered with this prestigious throng.

> "Blessed and holy is he that hath part in the first resurrection: on such the second death hath no power, but they shall be priests of God and of Christ, and shall reign with Him a thousand years" (Rev. 20:6).

b. The Second Resurrection

In prophecy, the first and second resurrections are usually mentioned together as we observe from the following passages:

> "And many of them that sleep in the dust of the earth shall awake, some to everlasting life, and some to shame and everlasting contempt" (Dan. 12:2).

> "Marvel not at this: for the hour is coming, in the which all that are in the graves shall hear His voice, and shall come forth; they that have done good, unto the resurrection of life; and they that have done evil, unto the resurrection of damnation" (John 5:28,29).

Although it may appear that the second resurrection follows directly on the heels of the first, Revelation 20:5 reveals otherwise. *"But the rest of the dead lived not again until the thousand years were finished. . . ."* This passage clearly indicates that there is a one thousand year *interlude* between these two events. After the close

174

of the millennial reign of Christ, Paul goes on to explain in I Cor. 15:24-26: *"Then cometh the end, when He shall have delivered up the kingdom to God, even the Father; when He shall have put down all rule and all authority and power. For He must reign, till He hath put all enemies under His feet. The last enemy that shall be destroyed is death [second resurrection]."*

The second resurrection includes *all* of the unsaved of all ages. They will be raised at the end of the millennium and be fitted with bodies capable of enduring everlasting punishment—a dreadful thought to say the least! These are the unbelieving who mocked God and persecuted the saints without mercy, but now *they* will be made to stand before our Lord at the Great White Throne.

The Apostle John writes these words in Rev. 20:12: *"And I saw the dead, small and great, stand before God; and the books were opened: and another book was opened, which is the book of life: and the dead were judged out of those things which were written in the books, according to their works."*

Beloved, as a pastor I have been frequently questioned by those perplexed by all of the violence in the world. Inquiring minds want to know, "Why doesn't God do something?" Believe me when I say: He will my friend, He will!

The above passage sets forth an awesome scene as John saw the dead, i.e., the spiritually dead, which are at enmity with God. He beheld both the destitute who had cursed God and the mighty kings who had denied His very existence. *"And the books were opened. . . ."* It appears that in addition to the records God so meticulously keeps of our works, these "books" would include the *Holy Scriptures,*

175

for God shall judge the unrighteous deeds of the ungodly according to His Word (Rom. 2:16).

"And another book was opened, which is the book of life...." Most believe, of course, that every time a sinner is saved his name is immediately recorded in the book of life. However, the Scriptures teach that *reservations* have been made for *everyone* before the foundation of the world. David writes in the Psalms under the direction of the Holy Spirit: *"Draw nigh unto my soul, and redeem it: deliver me because of mine enemies....mine adversaries are all before Thee.... Add iniquity unto their iniquity: and let them not come into Thy righteousness. Let them be blotted out of the book of the living, and not be written with the righteous"* (Psa. 69:18,19,27,28).

How could God blot out the names of David's enemies from the *book of life* if they were not there to begin with? You see, everyone's name, indeed, has been recorded there. Upon trusting Christ as our personal Savior our names are sealed there by the Holy Spirit until the day of redemption. But, if one rejects the gospel, and dies in his sins, his name is blotted out of the book of the living. Therefore, John says in Rev. 20:15:

> "And whosoever was not found written in the book of life was cast into the lake of fire."

When the angels open this book only a heartbreaking *blank space* will remain where the unbeliever's name once appeared. This will stand as a testimony against him, confirming that whosoever believeth not shall suffer eternal condemnation (John 3:18). This is the second death or eternal separation from God. He who is holy and righteous will have no other recourse than to cast all infidels into the Lake of Fire. His justice must be exercised to vindicate His holiness.

HELL will be everlasting destruction or loss of well-being. The lonely heart will *never* have the opportunity again to find its rest in God (II Thess. 1:9).

HELL will be the blackness of darkness forever (Jude 11-13). The inhabitants of this God-forsaken place will be gripped by an eerie darkness that will cause their souls to cry out, but there shall be no deliverance.

HELL will be an everlasting fire, where the flame is never quenched (Mark 9:42-46).

HELL will be weeping and gnashing of teeth. The unsaved will weep because they will realize it could have been different—*"If only I had believed!"* In all likelihood, the gnashing of teeth refers to their horrible anguish. May we also suggest that this could be the reaction of some to those who hastened their slide to this terrible torment. "You were the one who put that first bottle of liquor into my hand!" "You are the one who murdered me, cutting my life short—perhaps I would have believed!" (Matt. 25:30 cf. Acts 7:54; Rom. 2:5).

HELL will be spending eternity with devils, murderers, evildoers, sorcerers, and adulterers (Rev. 21:8).

HELL is *literal:* We beg of you to flee from the wrath of God to come before it is too late! May God help us, as never before, to have a burden for lost souls.

c. The Mystery and Our Resurrection

"Behold, I show you a mystery; We shall not all sleep, but we shall all be changed, In a moment, in the twinkling of an eye, at the last trump: for the trumpet shall sound, and the dead shall be raised incorruptible, and we shall be changed" (I Cor. 15:51,52).

Now the apostle takes under consideration *our* resurrection. Insofar as Paul was a member of the Body of Christ, it was necessary to change pronouns from "they" to "we" because he now turns his attention to our hope. *"We shall not all sleep."* One grand and glorious generation is going to escape death and be instantaneously changed and translated to glory. Preceding this moment of triumph, though, will be the resurrection of those Body members who have previously experienced death.

Henceforth, to help us distinguish this from the first resurrection we will refer to our resurrection as the *secret resurrection.* As we shall see, it pertains *only* to the members of the Body of Christ. Moreover, all of those who have died *in Christ* from the raising up of the Apostle Paul until the sound of the trump will be numbered with this *company* of saints.

There are two Scripture passages that substantiate this. First, when Paul comforts the saints at Thessalonica he reveals that those who ". . . believe that Jesus died and rose again. . ." will be raised at the Rapture. This is significant for this reason: These terms of salvation are *unique* to Paul's revelation, thus *limiting* the scope of this resurrection to the Church, the Body of Christ.

178

Second, in Phil. 3:11 the apostle states, *"If by any means I might attain unto the resurrection of the dead."* The word resurrection used here by the Holy Spirit is a compound noun (Gr. *exanastasis*) and literally denotes "the out-resurrection, out from among the dead." We should add that this term is only found here in the New Testament and is exclusively Pauline.

Paul's hope, as well as ours, is to be resurrected "out from the dead," i.e., from among the dead prophetic saints whom we mentioned before in few words. Thus, the *secret resurrection* is a *distinct* event and should never be confused with the first resurrection at the end of the Great Tribulation. The phrase *"If by any means I might attain"* is not an expression of doubt but rather one of humility. We believe the apostle is expressing that it was his desire to attain unto a *better* resurrection by living a sacrificial life for Christ (See Hebrews 11:35).

The resurrection shines as a beacon of hope to all of those who have placed their faith in Christ. We pray God will use these thoughts to challenge you to study anew this wonderful doctrine. To help the reader put the above in perspective, we trust that the following chart will be beneficial:

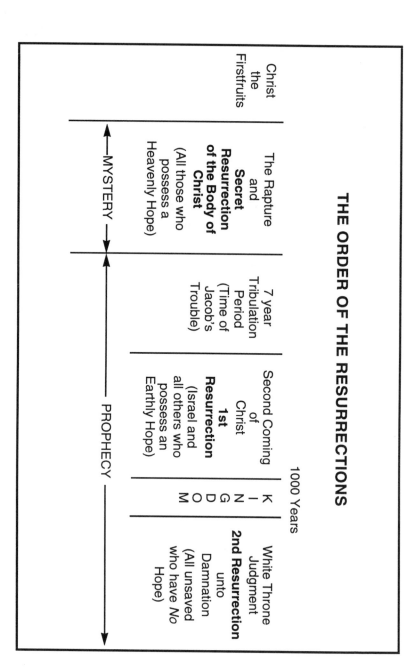

THE ORDER OF THE RESURRECTIONS

| Christ the Firstfruits | The Rapture and **Secret Resurrection of the Body of Christ** (All those who possess a Heavenly Hope) | 7 year Tribulation Period (Time of Jacob's Trouble) | Second Coming of Christ **1st Resurrection** (Israel and all others who possess an Earthly Hope) | 1000 Years K I N G D O M | White Throne Judgment unto Damnation **2nd Resurrection** (All unsaved who have *No* Hope) |

←—MYSTERY—→ ←——————— PROPHECY ———————→

11

The Realms Beyond Time

"It is appointed unto men once to die, but after this the judgment."

—Hebrews 9:27

Man has always had a curiosity about the unknown world beyond the grave. "What will tomorrow bring?" "Is there really life on the other side of the grave?" "Can there actually be an eternal judgment to come?" The world is searching for answers to these and many other questions concerning life after death. To add to their sense of uncertainty, there are now numerous reports from those who claim to have had a *near death experience.* These patients tell how they viewed every detail of their own resuscitation after being pronounced clinically dead. Disquieted by all of this, the unsaved consult their horoscopes, seers, mediums and the occult hoping to learn more about the future and what awaits them beyond the barrier of death.

On the other hand, the believer has at his disposal the infinite Word of God on such matters. Concerning "things to come" the Scriptures are the *only* source the child of God needs, since it is God who is the chief Architect of all the realms that transcend time.

CHRONICLES OF A DOCTOR

"There was a certain rich man, which was clothed in purple and fine linen, and fared sumptuously every day: And there was a certain beggar named Lazarus, which was laid at his gate, full of sores" (Luke 16:19,20).

181

Each writer of Holy Scripture brings his own personal characteristics to the pages of the Blessed Book. In the case of St. Luke, we are indebted to him for the meticulous detail he gives to, "...all that Jesus began both to do and teach." Being a physician, Luke would naturally have given attention to specifics due to the very nature of his vocation.

In Luke Chapter 16, Luke chronicles for us the *Parable of the Unjust Steward*. The audience our Lord was addressing was made up of His disciples along with a small group of Pharisees who had gathered inquisitively to take in His message. The *Parable of the Unjust Steward* primarily deals with the love of money, which is a root that is "all evil." In the eyes of some, bending the rules in order to have *fame* and *fortune* is worth the risk of being caught. Our Lord's parable *ends* at verse 13 at which time Luke carefully records the Pharisees' response to the Master's teaching. Needless to say, they were outraged that He would even imply that they were guilty of the same.

The Pharisees were members of the Sanhedrin, which was the Supreme Court of the land. Much like our own Supreme Court, the Pharisees were to interpret the Law not enact or alter it in any way. But this is exactly what they were guilty of! They had altered the Law of Moses to benefit their own cause, making themselves wealthy in the process. How they loved the praise of men!

The Lord peered straight into their hearts, exposing their unjust deeds and how they had even liberalized the boundaries of marriage and divorce to gain the favor of men (Ver. 18). They themselves were directly responsible for causing the Children of Israel to commit adultery, possibly

182

even some of *them* being guilty of the same. And what shall be the end of those who spurn the love of God and continue in their unrighteous ways? "There was a certain rich man...[who] lifted up his eyes, being in torments..." (Luke 16:19,23). Who was this rich man suffering in torment? Probably, he was a *former* Pharisee, who in life had fared sumptuously, having robbed God. But now he is consumed in terror until the day of judgment when he will receive his final sentence of doom. The Savior was warning this generation of hypocrites to flee the judgment to come lest they end up like their predecessor.

It has always been our conviction that Luke's account of the story of the "Rich Man and Lazarus" is a factual, literal chronicle of happenings in the *unseen world*. For a few moments in time, our Lord drew back the veil of the other realms that we might catch a glimpse of the activity that takes place in the spirit world. There are a number of reasons why this story is *not* a parable, but we will limit ourselves to the two main reasons.

First of all, a parable is defined as: "A placing beside . . . it signifies a placing of one thing *beside another* (my emphasis) with a view to comparison."[1] A good illustration of this is found in the gospel according to Matthew, where we have the parable of the *Wheat and Tares* (Matt. 13:24-30). When our Lord wanted to add to the disciples' understanding of the Kingdom, He simply placed a story like the *Wheat and Tares* (something they were familiar with) alongside a great kingdom truth. For example, we have the man who sowed the good seed in his field, but while he slept his enemy came and sowed tares among the

---

1. E. W. Vine, *Expository Dictionary of Old and New Testament Words*, Pg. 158.

wheat. When it was learned that this evil deed had been done, the servants were instructed to let both the wheat and tares grow together until the harvest.

Having His disciples' attention, the Master reveals by way of *comparison* that the man who sowed the good seed was the Son of Man. The field is the world, and the good seed (wheat) is the children of the kingdom. The enemy is the devil, who sowed the tares, which are representative of the children of the Wicked One. They are said to co-exist until the harvest, which is the end of the age (Matt. 13:36-43). The story of the *Rich Man and Lazarus* has *no such comparison*. Instead, we have a straightforward account like the verses that directly precede and follow it.

Secondly, in all of the parables our Lord spoke during His earthly ministry *never once* did He use a proper name. However, in Luke's description of the *Story of Dives (the Rich Man)*, no less than three proper names are made reference to, with all of whom we are well acquainted: Abraham, Lazarus and Moses. Much more could be said, but hopefully it is sufficient to say that before us in Luke Chapter 16 we have a startling view of the world of spirits.

THE UNSEEN WORLD

> "And in hell [hades] he lifted up his eyes, being in torments, and seeth Abraham afar off, and Lazarus in his bosom" (Luke 16:23).

When the rich man died he was carried by the angels of God to a place called *hades* which is located in the *center* of the earth (Psa. 63:9; Matt. 11:23; Matt. 12:40 cf. Acts 2:27). You will note from the above passage that the rich man is said to be "in hell" where he lifted up his eyes. It is of the utmost importance for the reader to understand at this point that Luke is *NOT* describing the terrors of the literal *hell* of the Bible, "Where their worm dieth not, and the fire is not quenched" (Mark 9:44).

We should pause here for a moment to comment that there is a *vast* difference between the Gr. *hades* (unseen world) and the Gr. *gehenna* (hell). Possibly you are thinking, "but I'm not a Greek scholar!" That's the wonderful thing about it; you don't have to be a scholar. We need only to consult those who have a knowledge of the original languages (God's gifts to the Church) in these problem areas. When the translators came to passages such as Luke 16:23 they found themselves in a *real dilemma.* What were they to do with the rich man, who they knew was in "hades" according to the original language, but were unable to directly translate this word because there is *no* English equivalent? They had one of two choices: don't translate it, leaving the space blank which, of course, would be totally unacceptable *or* find a word in the English language that at least had some similarity. Thus, they selected the word "hell" from our vocabulary, which falls far short of the intended meaning of the original Greek word "hades." Were the translators wrong in their choice? By no means, we believe they had no other alternative.

When we consult the original language we learn that the rich man, while in torment, was NOT in hell, which was—and is—yet future (Rev. 20:11-15). Instead, we are to understand that he was in "hades," which was the place of departed spirits. Hades, at the time of Luke's chronicle, as we previously mentioned, was located in the heart of the earth and was divided into *two compartments.* One

185

compartment comprised *paradise,* where all of the spirits of the departed saved awaited the coming of the Redeemer (Psa. 16:10; 139:8; Luke 23:39-43; Acts 2:27). The paradise section is also referred to as "Abraham's bosom," which denotes that it was a place of rest, security and blessing.

Between the *paradise* compartment and the *torment* section of hades, there was a great gulf fixed (Luke 16:26). This is doubtless a reference to the *bottomless pit* (Gr. *Abussos)* where the Antichrist is said to ascend out of after he is assassinated. Apparently, somewhere on the side of the Abyss there is a place called *tartarus* (Greek) where the angels who sinned in the days of Noah are chained (II Peter 2:4 cf. Isa. 14:15). The *torment* compartment of *hades* is where the rich man, along with all the other unsaved of all ages, await the future judgment to come (Psa. 9:17; 18:5; Matt. 11:23).

Although the torment of hades is very real it is not exactly the same intensity as the torment the unsaved will experience in the *Lake of Fire* to come. I say this because those in hades at this hour are all suffering the *same degree* of torment, having not yet been judged according to their works. However, *after* the White Throne Judgment those who are consigned to *hell* will suffer degrees of torment according to their evil deeds (Matt. 11:20-24; Rev. 20:12,13). In addition, the flame of hades is NOT eternal; it will one day be extinguished as God purges this old earth with fire, returning it to its pristine beauty wherein will dwell righteousness (II Peter 3:12,13).

186

THE LITERAL HELL

"But I say unto you, that whosoever is angry with
his brother without a cause shall be in danger of the
judgment: and whosoever shall say to his brother,
Raca, shall be in danger of the council: but whosoever shall say, Thou fool, shall be in danger of hell
[Gehenna] fire" (Matt. 5:22).

The Lord most frequently warned of the danger of *hell*
than any other who proclaimed the gospel in the New Testament. He wanted men to be well aware that if they rejected
the counsel of God against themselves they would one day
find themselves faced with the terrors of the Lake of Fire.

God *originally* created *hell* for the devil and his angels
(Matt. 25:41). This extreme measure was taken by God to
stop the defection of the angelic host to the ranks of Satan.
The pronouncement was made in heaven that those
angels who followed Satan in his rebellion would be consigned to eternal torment in the Lake of Fire with abso-
lutely *no* hope of reprieve. This action ended the rebellion
in short order, with only one-third of the angels siding
with the archenemy of God (Rev. 12:3,4,9).

Would you say that sin, rebellion, Satan and hell could
be said to be good, much less, *very good?* Without a
moment's hesitation, I am sure you would respond, "Ab-
solutely not!" When God completed His creative acts in
the beginning, He surveyed His creation and, ". . .saw
every thing. . .was *very good.* . . " (Gen. 1:31). Unquestionably, this indicates that Satan fell sometime between
Genesis 1:31 and Genesis 3:1, which means that *hell* was
also created during this same time period. A short time
later when Adam yielded to temptation and fell into sin,

187

he placed *himself,* along with the entire human race, in jeopardy of the *hellfire* judgment to come.

May I suggest that the location of hell (gehenna), or the Lake of Fire, seems to be fixed by our Lord as being somewhere in the distant reaches of the universe known as outer darkness (Matt. 8:12; 22:13; 25:30). The fires of this forbidding place are eternal and shall *never* be extinguished (Mark 9:42-48). At this hour, *not one soul* has yet been cast into hell as stated in Rev. 20:11-15. The first occupants of this inferno will be the Antichrist and the False Prophet who are cast alive into the fire at the close of the tribulation period (Rev. 19:20). As noted earlier, it is enough to cause one to tremble when we witness that 1,000 years later, the Antichrist and the False Prophet are *still* suffering in torment when the devil and his angels are cast there (Rev. 20:10).

In addition, the unsaved of all ages will be summoned out of *hades,* at which time they will *all* be required to stand before Christ at the *Great White Throne* (Rev. 20:11-15). One by one, the unbelievers will be judged to determine their degree of punishment in the eternal flame. They then will be taken to the mouth of *hell* that yawns before them and be cast into everlasting darkness to be remembered no more (Rev. 20:15).

Such a scene should cause us to plead with our friends and loved ones to believe on the Lord Jesus Christ before it is too late. It is our responsibility to warn them to flee this eternal calamity to come. Tell them that God loves them and that Christ, the Savior, died for their sins. But they must take heed that if they spurn the love of God and reject Christ as their personal Savior. He will one day be their Judge!

188

THE UNSEEN WORLD OF THE DEAD

HADES BEFORE THE CROSS

HEAVEN—THE ABODE OF GOD

Uninhabited

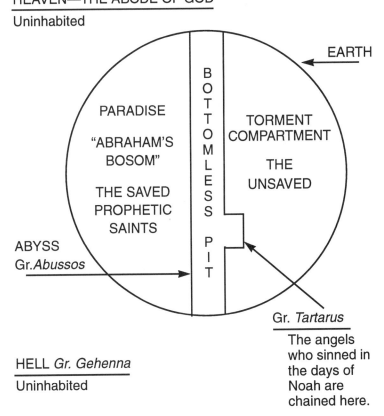

EARTH

PARADISE

"ABRAHAM'S BOSOM"

THE SAVED PROPHETIC SAINTS

B O T T O M L E S S P I T

TORMENT COMPARTMENT

THE UNSAVED

ABYSS
Gr.*Abussos*

Gr. *Tartarus*

The angels who sinned in the days of Noah are chained here.

HELL *Gr. Gehenna*

Uninhabited

THE UNSEEN WORLD OF THE DEAD
HADES AFTER THE CROSS

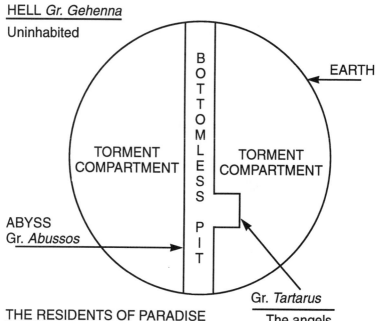

HELL *Gr. Gehenna*
Uninhabited

EARTH

B
O
T
T
O
M
L
E
S
S
P
I
T

TORMENT COMPARTMENT

TORMENT COMPARTMENT

ABYSS
Gr. *Abussos*

Gr. *Tartarus*

THE RESIDENTS OF PARADISE

1. The Prophetic Saints *temporarily* reside in heaven until the kingdom reign of Christ.

2. Members of the Body of Christ are permanent residents of the heavenly realm.

The angels who sinned in the days of Noah are chained here.

THE ETERNAL STATE

<u>HEAVEN—THE ABODE OF GOD</u>

INHABITANTS OF NEW HEAVEN

Members of the Body of Christ

NEW EARTH

INHABITANTS

Israel and
The Prophetic Saints

The Abolition of
Sin and Death

HADES WILL BE NO MORE!

<u>HELL Gr. *Gehenna*</u>

INHABITANTS:
The Devil and his Angels
The Unsaved of all Ages

OUR INHERITANCE

"Giving thanks unto the Father, which hath made us meet [fit] to be partakers of the inheritance of the saints in light:

"Who hath delivered us from the power of darkness, and hath translated us into the kingdom of His dear Son:

"In whom we have redemption through His blood, even the forgiveness of sins" (Col. 1:12-14).

Before we can follow the instructions of the Apostle Paul to render *thanks* unto God for our *inheritance* in the kingdom of His dear Son, we must first comprehend the phrase. Philip's words to the Ethiopian eunuch seem so apropos: "Understandest thou what thou readest?" A prayerful desire to understand will give us a deeper appreciation of these bountiful blessings which we have received from the hand of our heavenly Father.

When we take up the subject of the *kingdom,* there arises in the minds of most believers a sense of real frustration. This is due in part to the failure of pastors and teachers to rightly divide the Word of truth. The phrases in question are as follows: the kingdom of God, the kingdom of heaven, the kingdom of His dear Son, the heavenly kingdom and the kingdom of Christ. Unfortunately, most Bible teachers have taken these references to the *kingdom* and have tossed them into the air and they have come down mixed up like tossed salad.

To help alleviate the problem, we want to begin by making some general observations about the Kingdom of God. Hopefully, the following diagram will prove to be helpful in our search for the truth.

THE KINGDOM OF GOD IS OVER ALL

Prophecy	*The Mystery*
The House of Israel	The Body of Christ
"Kingdom"	"Heavenly Kingdom"
"Kingdom of Heaven"	"Kingdom of Christ"
12 Apostles	One Apostle, Paul
Hope: *Earthly*	Hope: *Heavenly*

The word "kingdom," much like the word "church," is a general term that must always be qualified by the context. For example, if someone should inquire, "Where do you believe the church is taught in the Word of God?" Our response would be: *"Which church?"* The kingdom of God is much the same; we must ask which aspect of the kingdom is in question.

Since the kingdom of God is over all it can be correctly said that *all* believers of all ages are under its government. Thus, as we have demonstrated in the above diagram when this phrase is used it *must* always be determined which program of God is in view—Prophecy or the Mystery.

a. Prophecy and the Kingdom of God

In prophecy, the phrases *kingdom of God* and *kingdom of heaven* are synonymous and oftentimes are used interchangeably. This is substantiated for us by comparing the gospels of Matthew and Mark which both introduce the reader to the beginning of our Lord's public ministry in Galilee.

> "Now when Jesus had heard that John was cast into prison, He departed into Galilee. . . . From that time Jesus began to preach, and to say, Repent: for the kingdom of heaven is at hand" (Matt. 4:12,17).

> "Now after that John was put in prison, Jesus came into Galilee, preaching the gospel of the kingdom of God, and saying, The time is fulfilled, and the kingdom of God is at hand: repent ye, and believe the gospel" (Mark 1:14,15).

Based upon our Lord's earthly ministry, it can be safely concluded that the kingdom of God in the Prophetic Scriptures refers to the earthly establishment of His kingdom and is tantamount to the 1,000 year reign of Christ. Furthermore, it is called the "kingdom of heaven" because the Lord will receive it from His Father in heaven and establish it here upon the earth (Luke 19:11,12; John 14:1-6). On that day, it literally will be like heaven upon the earth. According to Isaiah 35:1,6,8 the curse will be lifted ". . . *and the desert shall rejoice, and blossom as the rose. . . . Then shall the lame man leap as an hart, and the tongue of the dumb sing. . . . And an highway shall be there, and a way, and it shall be called The way of holiness."*

The house of Israel still anticipates the fulfillment of these prophecies when her Messiah will break through the heavens in a blaze of glory and conquer His enemies! In Christ's Second Coming, He will overthrow the kingdoms of the world and establish His own kingdom of peace and righteousness. Then, the dead shall come forth in the first resurrection and be ushered into the millennium where the 12 Apostles will sit upon 12 thrones judging the 12 tribes of Israel. Little wonder the Lord taught Israel to pray, ". . . *Thy kingdom come. Thy will be done in earth, as it is in heaven."*

194

b. The Mystery and the Kingdom of God

Did you notice the word "translated" in Col. 1:13? Believers today are *"translated into* the kingdom of [God's] dear Son." Where is the kingdom? In heaven, vested in the exiled King. And we are now "translated into" His kingdom. God has "made us fit to be partakers" of this glorious "inheritance of the saints in light."

Before the events of prophecy can come to pass, God will first bring to completion His plans and purposes for the Body of Christ. We also play an integral part in the kingdom of God but in a completely different sense than the house of Israel. God is doing something uniquely different among the Gentiles during the administration of Grace. Therefore, it is important to acknowledge that a dispensational change has taken place with the raising up of the Apostle Paul.

> "But none of these things move me, neither count I my life dear unto myself, so that I might finish my course with joy, and the ministry, which I have received of the Lord Jesus, to testify the gospel of the grace of God. . . . And now, behold, I know that ye all, among whom I have gone preaching the kingdom of God, shall see my face no more" (Acts 20:24,25).

Paul also preached the kingdom of God, but he taught it from the standpoint of a new program called the Mystery which as we know embodies the *heavenly* ministry of Christ (Rom. 16:25; Eph. 1:19-23; 2:1-7). With our attention focused on the heavenlies, in Paul's epistles we learn that the Body of Christ has a heavenly hope and calling.

Everyone knows that Chicago is a major metropolitan city located in the Midwest. It is a *place* where people live

195

and do business. In like manner, *heaven* is a tangible realm where the righteous will spend eternity with the Lord. Since our citizenship is in heaven, we have certain rights and privileges that flow from our position *in Christ.* In this regard, Paul's letter to the Ephesians brings us to the very *summit* of the revelation of the Mystery. From this vantage point, it is possible to see several points of interest as we look out over the riches of God's grace. Thus, we have been blessed with all *spiritual blessings* in heavenly places—chosen in Christ, predestinated unto the adoption of sons, accepted in the Beloved, forgiven, given an *inheritance,* sealed and seated with Christ in the heavenlies (Eph. 1:3-14). Like the splendor of the Rocky Mountains, the grace of God should never cease to amaze us!

Paul writes these words to Timothy, and to us as well, that we should have a confident expectation to be delivered, whether by death or Rapture, into the *heavenly kingdom:*

> "And the Lord shall deliver me from every evil work, and will preserve me unto His heavenly kingdom: to Whom be glory for ever and ever. Amen" (II Tim. 4:18).

We should add that the kingdom of God is not merely food and drink as some have supposed, but it is righteousness and peace and joy in the Holy Spirit. It is not in word as the Apostle says, but in power! (Rom. 14:17; I Cor. 4:20).

Thanks be unto God that we have been translated into the kingdom of God's dear Son! What joy to know that we are partakers of the inheritance with the saints in light.

196

We Gather Together

We gather together to ask the Lord's blessing,
  He chastens and hastens His will to make known;

The wicked oppressing now cease from distressing:
  Sing praise to His name—He forgets not His own.

Beside us to guide us, our God with us joining,
  Ordaining, maintaining His kingdom divine;

So from the beginning the fight we were winning:
  Thou, Lord, was at our side—all glory be Thine!

—Dutch Folk Song

197

12

The Judgment Seat of Christ

"But why dost thou judge thy brother? or why dost
thou set at naught thy brother? for we shall all stand
before the Judgment Seat of Christ."

—Romans 14:10

Life is full of appointments. They are a necessary part
of every business day and without them confusion would
reign supreme. Sometimes due to scheduling conflicts, an
appointment has to be canceled. I don't know about you,
but I for one always take great joy in changing my dental
appointment. Usually I can think of ten other things I'd
rather be doing. Be that as it may, there is one appointment we *will* honor, a divine one! Before the foundation of the world, God ordained a day when every believer
will be required to *appear* before the *Judgment Seat of
Christ.*

The subjects of this solemn event are *solely* members of
the Body of Christ. As we shall see, the sin question is not
the issue at this particular judgment. The purpose of the
Bema Seat is to ". . . make manifest the counsels of the
hearts: and then shall every man have praise of God"
(I Cor. 4:5). Few will dispute that the life of the Apostle
Paul exemplifies *how* to live a godly life in Christ Jesus.
Yet, even Paul looked upon *that day* with tremendous rev-
erence. We fear, however, that many in our day take this
matter far too lightly.

199

Some seem to think because we are "seated in the heavenlies" that the Judgment Seat of Christ is merely a formality. Here we must distinguish between our *standing* and our *state*. When it is said that we are "seated with Christ," this is our *standing,* which never changes since it is wholly dependent upon Christ. On the other hand, a constant vigilance must be kept to maintain our *state*. It can and does change based on our *actions*. Thus, our reigning position with Christ will be determined by our "present conduct." So how we live for Christ *now* will have a profound effect upon us throughout eternity.

THE PURPOSE OF THE BEMA SEAT

> "For we must all appear before the Judgment Seat of Christ; that every one may receive the things done in His Body, according to that he hath done, whether it be good or bad" (II Cor. 5:10).

The apostle teaches the *Judgment Seat of Christ* in both his early and later epistles. But it is of special interest to us that he deals more extensively with this subject in the *Corinthian* letters. The apparent reason for this was that the Corinthians had become *unfaithful* to the Lord. They were carnal and living in sin. Paul knew that they were in grave danger of suffering loss and, therefore, confronted them with their backslidden condition. He warned them night and day with tears that their infidelity would become unprofitable to them at *that day.*

The resemblance between the Church today and the Corinthian assembly is alarming. Nowadays, ungodly behavior prevails in the form of immorality, envy, strife and divisions. But what adds insult to injury is that those who know better *tolerate* it. To their credit, the

Corinthians turned from their carnality and were restored to the faith. Will the Church of our era follow suit or continue to trod down the path of unwholesome conduct? The closing lines of the story are yet to be written.

Throughout Paul's writings, it is evident that he was very familiar with the Greek culture. The phrase "judgment seat" in the above passage is derived from the Greek *Bema*. The *Bema* was a raised platform from which the judges presided over the Isthmian games. From this vantage point, the judges were in clear view of the spectators when they disqualified a participant or presented the victory garlands. In like fashion, Christ will appear in exaltation to *review* every believer's life and respond accordingly.

We should pause here to comment that it is conceivable for one judge to preside over two different types of proceedings. For example, a criminal court *magistrate* might hand down a death penalty to a convicted murderer. This same judge may also be called upon to oversee the summer Olympics. Here he enforces the rules of the games, making sure there is a level playing field as we say. Upon the completion of each event, he bestows the victory ribbons to the winners. Surely, the same could be said of our Lord; He, too, holds a dual judgeship.

Insofar as the *White Throne Judgment,* Christ will be the righteous Judge who condemns sinners to the second death. At that day, all *unbelievers* who rejected Christ as their personal Savior will be sentenced to the Lake of Fire for eternity. But He is also the one who presides over the "believers' judgment" when the roll is called up yonder (II Tim. 4:8). As mentioned earlier, the Judgment Seat of

201

Christ is not an accounting of our sins, for we are *forgiven* in Him. We have passed from death into life. Thus, we can confidently say:

> "There is therefore now no condemnation to them which are in Christ Jesus. . ." (Rom. 8:1).

Inasmuch as the sin question has been satisfied at Calvary, the purpose of the *Bema Seat* is to determine whether or not we were *faithful* to the Lord that bought us. The basis for this examination will be the *gospel of the grace of God.* Did we acknowledge Paul's apostleship? Were we *faithful* to proclaim Christ according to the revelation of the Mystery? Did we walk worthy of our calling? But what about those who have never known Paul's gospel? To this we say, the Judge of the earth shall do right. Our Lord is a fair and impartial Judge who will only hold us accountable for the light that we possessed. The greater danger lies with those who rejected the *Mystery* for the sake of positions, popularity, gain or the fear of men. Surely, the Lord will hold such responsible for their actions. This is heartbreaking, indeed, for their hearers were never given the opportunity to hear the *truth.*

THE MASTERBUILDER

> "For we are laborers together with God: ye are God's husbandry, ye are God's building. According to the grace of God which is given unto me, as a wise masterbuilder, I have laid the foundation, and another buildeth thereon. But let every man take heed how he buildeth thereupon" (I Cor. 3:9,10).

When Paul received his apostleship, it involved numerous responsibilities, one of which was *masterbuilder.* In other words, he was the chief architect who received the *blueprints* for this present dispensation from the Lord of Glory. Paul laid the foundation according to the *heavenly ministry* of Christ (I Cor. 3:11 cf. Eph. 1:19-23). Upon it is to be erected "grace building materials" that are only supplied for us in the Pauline epistles. Great care must be taken to follow the masterbuilder's plans in order that our *workmanship* and *service* will be well-pleasing to the Lord.

Perhaps a hypothetical case will help the reader understand the importance of the above paragraph. Let's suppose for a moment that a wealthy man secures an architect to build a two-story house. Since he is leaving town, he gives the architect the specifications and instructs him to purchase the site and secure a contractor. The owner's demands are carried out to the letter by the architect who then turns the project over to the contractor. But the contractor dislikes building two-story homes. He is convinced that the owner will be just as pleased with a ranch home. So, he discards the original blueprints and follows another set of plans.

Now I ask you, when the owner *returns* will he be pleased with the outcome? Obviously, he is going to require a full accounting from the builder as to why he didn't follow the plans of the architect. The owner is well within his rights to demand that the structure be torn down and rebuilt at the builder's expense. If we turn this to the spiritual side, the foregoing illustration raises a valid question. Will the Lord be pleased with those who have pushed aside Paul's blueprint to follow another gospel? Whether this is done wittingly or unwittingly due to the fear of men, their *loss* shall be great.

THE TEST

> "Now if any man build upon this foundation gold, silver, precious stones, wood, hay, stubble; Every man's work shall be made manifest: for the day [the day of Christ—Phil. 1:3-6] shall declare it, because it shall be revealed by fire; and the fire shall try every man's work of what sort it is" (I Cor. 3:12,13).

The apostle makes it very clear that there are two distinct groups of materials that can be used by those who build on his foundation. Although these instructions were originally intended for pastors and teachers, Paul also meant them to be applied by *every* member of the Body of Christ. The first grouping of materials (gold, silver and precious stones) represents those things that are done in accordance with Paul's gospel. It is discovering what the doctrines of grace *are, standing* for them uncompromisingly, and making an *application* of them in our daily lives.

If we have a burden for lost souls and faithfully make known the *Commission of Reconciliation,* which *excludes* the rite of water baptism—that's gold, silver and precious stones (II Cor. 5:12-21 cf. Col. 2:9-17). Interestingly, this particular grouping is found *in* the earth and must be excavated with much *effort* and at substantial *cost.* Anyone who champions the *cause of grace* can relate to this last statement. Furthermore, to a greater or lesser degree, this trio is *refined* when passed through the flame. Thus, gold, silver and precious stones signify the *permanent* nature of our *works* that are done according to the Pauline master plan.

The second group of building materials are found on the *surface* of the earth. Thus, they are *temporal.* These

204

works (wood, hay and stubble) will perish when they are passed through the flame. Those who have spent a lifetime adding Petrine doctrines to the Pauline foundation will see their efforts go up in smoke at the Judgment Seat of Christ. As sincere as they may be, they are sincerely *wrong!* We are in no way downplaying the earthly ministry of Christ. Quite the contrary, the kingdom gospel is a wonderful truth, but it is NOT God's message for today!

Please consider this prayerfully for the basic premise of the *Great Commission* involves the following: *Repentance,* that is, for breaking the covenant of the Law and crucifying the Messiah (Luke 3:7-14 cf. Acts 2:22,23,38); *Believe* that Jesus is the Christ (Messiah of Israel), the very Son of God (Mark 16:16 cf. John 20:31), and declare *water baptism* for the remission of sins (Mark 1:4; 16:16 cf. Acts 2:38). Then from the lips of the Lord Himself:

"And these signs [miraculous manifestations] shall follow them that believe; In my name shall they cast out devils; they shall speak with new tongues; They shall take up serpents; and if they drink any deadly thing, it shall not hurt them; they shall lay hands on the sick, and they shall recover" (Mark 16:17,18 cf. Acts 2:4; 3:6-9; 5:29-31).

Is this the commission we are to carry to a lost and dying world today? Obviously not! In addition, wood, hay and stubble may also take the form of liberalism, legalism, the teaching of self-esteem, new evangelicalism, Covenant Theology, etc. Any *ism* or *schism* that does not align itself with Paul's blueprints will result in terrible *loss* at that day. If you have been pondering what men may say if you accept the *grace message,* perhaps the more pertinent question is: What will the Lord say if you don't?

205

It is a solemn thought that "every man's work shall be made manifest." The word "manifest" here stands out like the *Statue of Liberty* in New York harbor for the day of Christ will *declare* the very *intent* of our heart. Each and every work will be tested by *fire* (I Cor. 3:13). *Fire* in the Scriptures is used in various senses, but in this context it symbolizes the *Word of God.* The reader will recall when Jeremiah sought to flee from the presence of the Lord that God's Word was ". . . as a *burning fire* shut up in my bones" (Jer. 20:9). "All Scripture is given by inspiration of God. . .," but it must be interpreted in light of Paul's revelation. Consequently, our works will be tested by Paul's epistles, since they set forth the *commands of Christ* for us today (I Cor. 14:37).

Moreover, every believer's work will be tested as to what *sort* it is. Some go about trying to impress others with how much they have accomplished. But God is more concerned about *quality,* not quantity. The man who proudly opens his little black book to show how many he led to Christ may be in for a rude awakening. Imagine his surprise when the Lord inquires as to how many of these he grounded in the gospel of the grace of God! Our present commitment to Christ, or lack thereof, will have a lasting effect on three specific areas of our eternal state.

THE RECOMPENSE OF REWARD

Last year at this time, a Brinks truck was traveling down one of our Chicago expressways when the unexpected happened. Apparently, the driver had forgotten to secure the rear doors properly which set up an interesting chain of events. As the truck rounded a sharp bend in the road, the back doors flew open and huge bags of money began cascading into oncoming traffic. It might seem rather strange to some that the operator of the vehicle was unaware that his precious cargo was being distributed on the street behind him. But in Chicago, traveling on the interstates can be a life-threatening experience. Lane changes are often made at high speed with only inches to spare between the vehicles. Driving here is not for the fainthearted! It requires your undivided *attention* if you hope to survive to the next exit.

Well, after a long day, the driver arrived safely at the depot in Indiana. However, there was one small problem: Most of the money he was hauling was missing! Back on the expressway, motorists thought that "their ship had come in" as they gathered up bundles of currency from the roadway. Now they were faced with the biggest decision of their lives: Cast morality to the wind and keep it, or return their new found fortune that did not rightfully belong to them. I believe it was Martin Luther who said, "It is a dangerous thing to disobey your conscience." That evening, most of the money was returned to the authorities by law-abiding citizens who felt it was the right thing to do. Of course, they were handsomely *rewarded* for their honesty.

The same can be said of the Christian life. God has saved us according to the *riches* of His grace and has called us with a holy calling. If we faithfully serve the Lord and *return* to Him the honor and glory that is rightfully due Him, He will *reward* us accordingly. Our faithfulness *now* will have a bearing upon us throughout eternity. Thus, it is essential for us to be *obedient* even in the seemingly small things. Probably it seemed like such a small thing when the Lord said to Lot and his wife ". . . *look not behind thee. . ."* (Gen. 19:17). But when Lot's wife turned to gaze upon the fiery destruction of those cities of the plain, she suffered severe consequences for her actions. She was turned into a pillar of *salt!* God desires that we be faithful in *all things* so that we might reap the full *recompense of reward.*

a. Rewards

"If any man's work abide which he hath built thereupon, he shall receive a reward. If any man's work shall be burned, he shall suffer loss: but he himself shall be saved; yet so as by fire" (I Cor. 3:14,15).

Those who build upon Paul's foundation with gold, silver and precious stones are promised a *reward* for their faithful service. Exactly what form this may take we are not told; whatever God has in store for us is sure to be a blessing. Therefore, it is in our interest to obey the counsel of His will. Rewards will also be given in the form of *crowns.* Here we must distinguish between the *kingly crown* of prophecy and the *victor's crown* found frequently, though not solely, in Paul's revelation. The royal *diadem* is closely associated with the millennial *kingship* of Christ, whereas the *stephanos* speaks of the *victory garland* that was bestowed upon those who were victorious in a particular sporting event. It is this latter *crown* that is said by Paul to be bestowed on the *faithful* at the Judgment Seat of Christ. Whether or not these are literal crowns that will be given at that day is doubtful. We do know, however, that they represent specific areas of the believer's walk that will be *acknowledged* by the Savior.

208

"For what is our hope, or joy, or *crown of rejoicing?* Are not even ye in the presence of our Lord Jesus Christ at His coming? For ye are our glory and joy" (I Thes. 2:19, 20). This is the soul winner's crown. Paul could confidently say that he was "pure from the blood of all men" (Acts 20:26). In other words, everywhere the apostle set foot he told men about the meritorious work of Christ. Thus, those who labor sacrificially that others might hear the gospel will receive special *recognition* for having compassion on the lost.

"And every man that striveth for the mastery is temperate in all things. Now they do it to obtain a corruptible crown; but we an *incorruptible [crown]*" (I Cor. 9:25). The athlete who is training for a particular event exercises *self-control* in all things that he might perform to his maximum ability. In the spiritual arena, those who desire to bring their bodies under *subjection* must also apply the above principle. In so doing, they strive to have victory over the flesh by disciplining themselves to yield their members as instruments of righteousness. With every fiber of their being, they have glorified God. Insofar as they have successfully abstained from all appearance of evil, a very special honor will be bestowed upon them.

". . . I have finished my course, I have kept the faith: Henceforth there is laid up for me a *crown of righteousness,* which the Lord, the righteous judge, shall give me at that day: and not to me only, but unto all them also that love His appearing" (II Tim. 4:7,8). In spite of many obstacles, the Apostle Paul had finished his course with joy. And one of the contributing factors that enabled him to endure such hardships was the *blessed hope.*

209

When I was on the varsity track team in high school, Coach Humphreys required two things of every member of the track team. First, if you fell you were to get up and finish the race. You have no way of knowing, he would say, if the runner in first place will be disqualified. Second, you were to complete the race, even if in last place, in order to maintain a sense of accomplishment. In a nutshell, always finish what you start!

We, too, are in a race. The course is long, the hurdles many, but those who love His *appearing* will receive the *crown of righteousness*. Of course, some believers only look for the Lord's coming in times of crisis. Paul, however, has in mind the saint who lives every waking moment in anticipation of the Lord's *appearing*.

b. Reigning with Christ

"It is a faithful saying. . . If we suffer, we shall also reign with Him: if we deny Him, He also will deny us: If we believe not, yet He abideth faithful: He cannot deny Himself" (II Tim. 2:11-13).

Are we willing to suffer for Christ? If we are, then we shall also reign with Him; that is, to a *higher degree*. All believers shall rule and reign with Christ, but not all shall hold the same position. One need only read the history of the Reformation to see what terrible things the saints endured for the cause of Christ. Because they were willing to name the name of Christ, they suffered many barbaric injustices. The journal of the Reformation reads like a handbook on "How to Torture the Innocent." Those dear saints experienced everything from cruel mockings to being burned at the stake. Nevertheless, they obtained a

210

good report through *faith* and ensured themselves a *better* reigning position with Christ.

Many believers around the world still experience similar atrocities today. But here in America, the most common form of suffering is *rejection*. Whatever the form may be, if we are willing to *stand* for the truth, our Lord will look favorably upon us. But "if we deny Him, He also will deny us." Those who question the doctrine of eternal security often appeal to this passage as proof that if we are found unfaithful in the course of our Christian life, Christ will deny us salvation. Nothing could be further from the truth as the following passage confirms. *"If we believe not, yet He abideth faithful: He cannot deny Himself"* (II Tim. 2:13). The proper interpretation of the foregoing passage is: If we are *ashamed* of Christ, He will *deny* us a higher reigning position with Him because of our unfaithfulness. Yet He abideth faithful to His Word. Christ has promised *eternal life* to all those who believe on Him (Rom. 6:23). Inasmuch as God cannot lie, He *cannot* deny Himself (Titus 1:2).

It is the very nature of God to do everything decently and in order. This is clearly seen in relation to the angelic host. The seraphims are said to hover *above* the throne of God. Then, there are the cherubims who *encircle* the throne. The seven spirits stand *before* the presence of God prepared to carry out His highest commands at a moment's notice. Stepping down to the next order of angels, we have the *principalities* who hold the classification of *supreme rulers*. The *powers* are delegated by a general. The next rung down are the *thrones,* which are *seats* held by angelic beings over assigned *territories*. Then, there is

211

the realm of *dominions,* which are *divisions* under the thrones. Finally, we have the rank of *might* or the *enforcement agency* (Isa. 6:1-3; Ezk. 28:14 cf. Rev. 4:6-9; Rev. 4:5; Eph. 1:21 cf. Col. 1:16).

The archenemy of God has basically ordered his forces of evil in the same manner. At the present, they occupy the second heaven. But the time is soon coming when the devil and his angels shall be cast out of heaven to the earth (Rev. 12:7-10). Subsequently, the members of the Body of Christ shall assume the positions vacated by the fallen host. Little wonder Satan hates the Mystery. So then, our *present faithfulness* will determine the level of reigning position with Christ throughout eternity (Eph. 2:6,7).

c. The Resurrection

> "There is one glory of the sun, and another glory of the moon, and another glory of the stars: for one star differeth from another star in glory. So also is the resurrection of the dead. . ." (I Cor. 15:41,42).

Here the Apostle Paul draws an illustration from the heavens above to establish that there will be *degrees of glorification* in the future resurrection. As stated earlier, one does not need to be an astronomer to understand that the sun has a greater glory than the moon. The sun produces its own light which sustains life on the earth; therefore, it has a greater glory than all other heavenly bodies. On the other hand, the moon has a glory all its own as it rules the night. In addition, no two stars are alike. Some are larger than others. Some are brighter than others. Some are greater distances from the earth. Some stars form constellations such as the Big and Little

212

Dippers, while others like the North Star are used for navigational purposes.

By comparison, the apostle states, "so also is the resurrection of the dead." When God imparts to us our new bodies, they will greatly *differ* one from another. First, no two believers shall have the same appearance because our *identities* shall be preserved in the resurrection. Second, the degree that our bodies will be glorified is determined on the basis of whether or not we *walk worthy* of our calling. These degrees *may* manifest themselves in the following ways: a fuller knowledge, a greater mobility in the spiritual realm or increased responsibility. Even though God does not explain these varying degrees of glorification, whatever He has made known to us is worthy of our attention, especially since it will have a bearing upon us in the ages to come.

The Judgment Seat of Christ is in no way a beauty contest where Christ will capriciously show favor to some while passing by others. Some tend to look upon this judgment in that manner. The above areas are solely based upon our *individual conduct* and *faithfulness*. God has given us a lifetime of opportunities; if we suffer loss at that day, we will have no one to blame but ourselves.

The following story was told by a father who learned how unwise it was to neglect spending time with his son: "One year ago today, I sat at my desk with a month's bills and overdue accounts before me when my bright-faced young boy rushed in and impetuously announced, 'Happy birthday, Dad! Mom says you're 55 today, so I'm going to give you 55 kisses, one for each year.' He began to make good on his word when I exclaimed, 'Oh, Andy, not now;

I'm too busy!' He became silent, and when I looked up I saw that his big blue eyes were filled with tears. Apologetically I said, 'You can finish tomorrow.' He made no reply, but he was unable to conceal his disappointment as he quietly walked away. That same evening, I called to him. 'Come and finish those kisses now, Andy.' Either he didn't hear me or he wasn't in the mood for there was no response.

Two months later, as a result of an accident, God took him home to heaven. His body was laid to rest in a little cemetery near a place where he loved to play. The robin's note was never sweeter than my son's voice, and the turtledove that cooed to its nestlings was never so gentle as the little one who left unfinished his love-imposed task. If only I could tell him how much I regret those thoughtless words I spoke, and how my heart is aching now because of my unkind actions. Instead, I sit here thinking, 'Why didn't I return his love? Why did I grieve his young heart that was so full of tenderness and affection?'"[1]

A CLOSING THOUGHT

Regret is a terrible thing. We fear though that many at the Judgment Seat of Christ will look back over their lives only to *regret* that they failed to acknowledge Paul's apostleship and message. Perhaps a lifetime of turmoil could have been averted had they only accepted the *Word, rightly divided.*

---

1. *Windows on the Word,* Dennis J. De Haan, Compiler, Pg. 68.

"Only one life; 'Twill soon be past.

"Only what's done for Christ will last."

Are you living in light of the Rapture? Are you resting in the promises given to the Church? Are you *prepared* for the sound of the trump? Thanks be unto God that the members of the Body of Christ are partakers of His *eternal purpose* and, therefore, have been *delivered* from the wrath to come! Truly, this is the *Triumph of His Grace!*

223

THE BEREAN BIBLE SOCIETY

For over 50 years the *Berean Bible Society* has been "An Organization for the Promotion of Bible Study." Standing firm on the fundamentals of the Christian faith, it employs many means to interest people in the study of the Scriptures, among them the following:

BBS arranges *Bible Conferences* for the study of the Word. Its President, Paul Sadler, has spoken at many such conferences throughout the United States and Canada.

The Society publishes the *Berean Searchlight,* a Bible study magazine edited by Pastor Sadler, and sent free of charge to readers in every state in the Union and more than 60 foreign countries.

"Two Minutes With the Bible," a weekly newspaper column featured in hundreds of newspapers across the country is another means BBS uses to reach the masses with the Word. This column now has a weekly readership running into the millions.

Tape recorded messages are provided free of charge through our free lending library and for use in Bible classes. Some taped messages are offered for sale at modest prices.

BBS has been proclaiming the message of grace for many years through *radio broadcasts* in many parts of the country.

These growing ministries are carried on by the voluntary contributions of believers who desire to see others reached with the truths that have brought so much light and blessing to their own lives.

EXPLORING THE UNSEARCHABLE RICHES OF CHRIST

The Key That Unlocks The Sacred Secret

By
Paul M. Sadler

A comprehensive study in dispensational truth!

This volume takes a fresh new look at what we mean by the phrase "rightly dividing the Word of truth." The reader will find of interest that one whole chapter is devoted to *how* the ages and dispensations harmonize. Also, included are many helpful charts, dispensational graphs and a Scripture index.

190 PAGES

CLOTHBOUND   **GOLD STAMPED**

Order your copy today!

BEREAN BIBLE SOCIETY
7609 W. Belmont Ave.   Chicago, IL 60635

THE BEREAN SEARCHLIGHT

YOU CAN HELP GET THIS MESSAGE OUT TO OTHERS

Send for our free Bible Study Magazine and a full Price List of our Literature

BEREAN BIBLE SOCIETY

7609 W. Belmont Ave.   Chicago, IL 60635

CASSETTE TAPE RECORDINGS FOR FURTHERING YOUR UNDERSTANDING OF THE WORD, RIGHTLY DIVIDED BY PASTOR PAUL M. SADLER

1. *Heaven:* This album contains four-cassette tapes which describe the glories of the heavenlies.

2. *Prayer, Dispensationally Considered:* This three-cassette album focuses on the prayer life of the believer in the present administration of Grace.

3. *Pretribulational Rapture of the Church:* This album contains four-cassette tapes that are designed to help the child of God prepare for coming events.

4. *Understanding Dispensationalism:* This six-cassette album presents all of the dispensations in clear, understandable language.

5. *Hard Sayings of St. Paul:* This two-cassette album deals with some of the more difficult passages found in Paul's epistles.

6. *Dispensational Position of John's Writings:* This eight-cassette album primarily focuses on where the writings of the Apostle John fit into the overall scheme of things.

7. *Revelation, A Dispensational Introduction:* This album contains three-cassette tapes that are devoted to clearing up the confusion that often surrounds the early chapters of the Book of Revelation.

For a *free* Tape Catalog, simply write to: The *Berean Bible Society,* 7609 W. Belmont Ave., Chicago, IL 60635

NOTES

NOTES